The Music of Solid Objects

JOHN DICKSON

Illustrated by
John Clark

For more poetry books by John Dickson
Visit www.puddinheadpress.com

All Rights Reserved
Printed in the United States of America
First Edition
First Printing

THE MUSIC OF SOLID OBJECTS
By John Dickson
© 1997 by John Dickson

Cover Art: John Clark
"The Music of Solid Objects,"
permission given by the artist

Photography: Vicki Grayland

Manuscript design: Elizabeth Grudzien

ISBN: 0-939395-22-3
Library of Congress Catalog Number 97-061511

Published in 1997
Thorntree Press
547 Hawthorn Lane
Winnetka, IL 60093

acknowledgements

Grateful acknowledgment is give to these periodicals in which these poems appeared:

American Goat	Jean Sibelius
American Scholar	The Grapes of Wrath, Novelist
Chicago Literary Review	Queen Christina
Chicago Review	Modigliani, The White Gull and The Cows Fat Tongue
Elf	Paganini, The Troubadour Chronicles, Hart Crane, The Mortality of Stone
Hammers	Cezzane, Rembrandt, Diane Arbus, Georgio de Chirico
Images	Molly In The Kitchen, The Welchmen, Capricio, The Poet In the Cage, Isadora Duncan, Juan Ponce de Leon
Poetry	A Tale of Two Cities, After the Rubaiyat, Fugue
Karamu	Edwin Grauer Painting the Battle of San Michele, Wilhelm Freideman Bach
Pulpsmith	At the Grave of Maxwell Bodenheim
Mississippi Valley Review	The Painter
Jean's Journal	Delius
Salome	The Red Shoes
Without Halos	Matisse, Role Model Dream
Spoon River Quarterly	d.a. Levy, Subject Matter
Rhino	Henri de Toulouse Lautrec
Thorntree Anthology	Chagall
Wind Magazine	Glenn Miller

Contents

1	MOLLY IN THE KITCHEN
2	THOMAS WOLFE
3	LORENZ HART
5	THE WELCHMEN
6	THE GRAPES OF WRATH
8	PAGININI
9	CEZANNE
11	THE TROUBADOUR CHRONICLES
12	QUEEN CHRISTINA
13	ART GALLERY
15	MATISSE
16	AT THE GRAVE OF MAXWELL BODENHEIM
17	THE MORTALITY OF STONE
18	THE DAY GEORGE GERSHWIN DIED
20	HART CRANE
21	MAGRITTE
22	SHAKESPEARE
23	A TALE OF TWO CITIES
24	THE GARDEN OF LOVE
25	CHAGALL
27	REMBRANDT
28	REMBRANDT'S SON
29	SHERWOOD ANDERSON
30	THE NOVELIST
32	PETER BREUGEL
33	THE PAINTER
34	SUBJECT MATTER
37	DIANE ARBUS
38	MODIGLIANI
41	JAMES ENSOR
42	EDGAR DEGAS
43	WILHELM FRIEDEMANN BACH
45	LEONARDO DA VINCI
46	FRANZ LISZT
47	THE POET IN THE CAGE
50	VASLAV NIJINSKI
51	HENRI DE TOULOUSE LAUTREC
54	VINCENT VAN GOGH
55	DALI AND VAN GOGH
56	EDWIN GRAUER PAINTING THE BATTLE OF SAN MICHELE

58	GEORGE BERNARD SHAW
59	AFTER THE RUBAIYAT
60	GLENN MILLER
61	FUGUE
63	ITALIAN POETRY READING
64	DELIUS
66	JEAN SIBELIUS
67	REGINALD MARSH
68	SERGEI IN CONCERT
69	ROLE-MODEL DREAM
71	SERGEI ESENIN
72	THE LONG BOATS
73	MR. BECK'S'S BOOKSTORE
74	WINSTON CHURCHILL
76	ISADORA DUNCAN
78	GEORGIO DE CHIRICO
80	FRANK
82	"GUERNICA"
84	PABLO NERUDA
87	LUDWIG CON BRIO
88	THE WHITE GULL AND THE COW'S FAT TONGUE
90	d.a. levy
93	THE RED SHOES
94	ON READING THE LIFE OF JUAN PONCE DE LEON
96	CAPRICCIO
98	STREETS OF NOBLE BIRTH
101	EXCAVATION
102	POETRY READING

For Virginia.

PREFACE

It has been sad in a way, dealing with the biographies of creative people, because they invariably die in the end, even though their work lives on. Of course, this is not the case with autobiographies where the subject seldom, if ever dies. But as far as actual facts are concerned, autobiographers are tempted to show their lives as they wish they had been (or to present themselves as they consider themselves to be.) I have adhered to the more objective biographies than the occasionally tainted autobiographies — not to imply that the writing of an autobiography guarantees immortality. Sooner or later, I've discovered, even autobiographers learn they are as mortal as anyone else.

MOLLY IN THE KITCHEN

Read me your poem, go on,
read your poem to me so I can nestle
in the feel of it, bask in all the sounds of it
thinking of how Catullus and Cornelius
and all that young and bawdy gang
went reeling through the streets of Verona
after boisterous nights of reading their stuff,
so hooked on cadences of Latin,
Latin, their live and living language.
How they revelled in the ribaldry they aimed
at all the classic poems of war and conquest,
senators, centurions, and Caesar himself,
that greatest of all baldheaded emperors.

Or read as Frank O'Hara read,
the way he read his poem to Jane and Larry,
Grace and all his hundred thousand friends,
each poem a celebration for knowing them,
marking their lives, welding them all together.
Every line part of his life, his joy of it,
his zest for it, his screwed-up, driving loves.
His chosen heroes, Mayakovsky and Rachmaninoff.
His fascination, Second Avenue,
until that inconspicuous night on Fire Island
when he calmly wandered into violent death
holding them all forever in a past
that seemed like some great light, some Shangri-La
of his reading his poems or just being there.
As though he were the only past they ever had.

Just read as you always read,
not on stage,
not as Poe or Dylan, boozy in their taverns
or Neruda in the phosphate mines
or even Emily, who maybe never ever read at all.
Read as you always do,

your voice showing off,
each word saying, "Look what I've written,"
asking, "What do you think?"
turning me into the only boy
not locked away in the Pied Piper's mountain
turning me into an afternoon of rain on the windows,
no one out in the streets
and you in the kitchen reading your poem.

THOMAS WOLFE

Spawned from the mountains.
Conceived by the haunting penetration
of night and trains, of time and the river
in the egg of impassive cities of people.
Cursed with a frenzy to melt into words,
his pencil somehow attached to his brain.
Obsessed by the book that would be his life,
pouring in it every cow and barn
every tree and house and restaurant face,
every eye, every voice, every aspect of love,
scribbled out in majestic prose, in bad prose,
in violent, driven prose
that fed on coffee and cigarettes
and kept him shut in his New York room
pouring out a niagara of words
that matched the matrix of his blood
as he constantly molded The Book! The Book!

Cartons and crates of prolific pages,
but who in his right mind would publish it all?
Or read it? Or write it?
More of a recluse with each rejection,
more disheveled and wild-eyed
young and unshaven and growing fat
hating his mistress, berating his friends
and all the while The Book

like a cancer, growing. . .growing. . .
storing his avalanche of words.
Finally an editor cut it in half,
forced its pages between two covers,
spanked it to make it breathe
and held it up for the world to see.
The remnants took on a life of their own,
the hydra-headed, deathless book
that spewed out pages night and day
like lava smothering a village
as it boils its way to fill up the sea.

A recurring pain that took root in his head
began blotting him out in the middle of thoughts,
in the middle of words,
blotting out pages that lay on the floor
and slicing his life into small chunks.
Until doctors decided to ease the pressure,
to release the fluid gathered there
by drilling a hole in his skull,
a small hole ever so carefully,
then stood back in wonder as all his words
and all his pages and chapters and books
and mountains and rivers and valleys and trains
and voices crying in the night
spurted three feet into the air.

LORENZ HART

Rodgers and Hart. . .Rodgers and Hart. . .
everyone singing Rodgers and Hart.
I Married An Angel. . .My Funny Valentine. . .
And Suddenly My Heart Stood Still.

They met in college—Rodgers a teenager,
Hart a post-graduate, five feet tall,
looking a little like Al Capone.
Eternal cigar and built-up shoes.
Sometimes he'd have to shave twice a day.
Voracious reader of books, books,
Shakespeare and Fielding, Proust and Wolfe,
a head full of books that kept bleeding words
he could suddenly, magically turn into songs
that were backbone and soul for their Broadway shows.

His eyes were a stage. His brain was a pencil.
Women would fall in love with his words.
And he liked the Girl-and-Music shows
that surrounded him with dancing and singing.
America's Toulouse Lautrec.
The dancers loved him, but not *that* way,
made excuses based on his fat cigars.

He expected success, wept at bad reviews,
gave anyone money and bought all the drinks.
Then Pearl Harbor and all the men leaving.
Freida, his beloved mother, died
and he, forty-two, had still never married.
After Rodgers did "Oklahoma" with Hammerstein
he began to hide out, no one ever knew where,
just to keep from writing more songs.
"Where is he? We need him! Check all the bars!"
If they found him he'd dash off a song or two,
then disappear in the walls of the city.

Asked Vivienne Segal to marry him
and of course she loved him, but "not that way."
Soon a mixture of liquor and rain
brought on one more of his recent comas
and during a black-out alarm of New York
he died the way he would have staged it.

THE WELCHMEN

True or not, I know it to be a fact
that Dylan Thomas' *Collected Poems*
were buried in the box with Richard Burton,
that little comfort-blanket book a guarantee
he'd live forever, never leaving childhood nor Wales
as once below a time he ran his heedless ways
so young and easy under the new made clouds.
Bound by those words that Dylan wore like diamonds
to memories that were common to them both:
the foxes beyond the farm barking clear and cold,
the sailboats knocking on the net-webbed wall,
the bells rocking the hills. Even Captain Cat
haunted by all his long-ago drowned sailors
or Mog Edwards the draper so mad with love
for Miss Price and she saying, "Yes, Oh yes, yes,"
as all the bells of the tills of the town
rang for their wedding.

Dylan with fields of barley rooted in his brain
spewing his words, coaxing his words
of rain on the harbor, or milkmaids
gentle in their clogs over the fallen sky.
Dylan, intimate friend of Eve and Adam
writing in his shed in the yard, bathing in memories
of heron over St. John's Hill
or the woman crying, "What will the neighbors say?"
Drinking his words alive,
blaming time for strangling him
as Death stood at his shoulder all the time.

And Richard, born with a voice like a harp,
like a pine, like echoes in a cave,
constantly tickled by the rub of love,
a few drinks with tedious company
enough to take him back to a soot-stained pub.
Rousing Dylan's words, carousing his words,

eating his words, rolling them over his tongue,
like Bacchus with a beard of grapes, belching words
like goosefield, furze, or windfall light.
Loving as he'd act love; dying as he'd act death,
vital...young...exhausted...old...
singing his drunken songs,
the moon and its hills,
the river and its trees,
the whiskey and its words.

THE GRAPES OF WRATH

Steinbeck fights for discipline.
No more books of hate and rage
like the two he vomited up and burned
after visiting the migrant camp.
Dragged families from their flooded tents,
walked miles and back to bring them food
and saw ruined Oklahoma farmers starve,
actually dying as he watched!
Finally he begins the book
and a diary all in longhand, all in ink ,
two thousand words his daily goal.
Plays Tchaikovsky, plays Stravinsky
for the feel of it, to bring his characters to life.

> Show sun-baked fields. Parched earth. The dust.
> The sound of tractors, their smell of oil and heat.
> The phone rings. The doorbell rings.
> The radio blares too loud next door.
> Be objective. Keep the discipline.
> Fight the urge to shout...the urge to quit.
> Stay in control. Fight being angry.
> It's going well. It's going badly.
> Don't think largeness work from page to page.
> Remember to make the soil red, not grey.
> Keep Tom and Ma together. Have Grandpa die tomorrow.

The telephone. The visitors. A peddler at the door.
The flies and heat and rain. Carpenters pounding.
Hitler won't invade the Czechs.
Germans are much too nice for that.

Slow down! Slow down! The story is growing.
Crippled cars line Route 66,
loose bearings, shattered tires, broken springs.
A gasket blows. The kids want water.
One hundred pages, near exhaustion.
Discipline the writing, the words, the language.
Two hundred pages, celebration.
It's moving along. It's falling apart.
Three hundred pages: it's no use! Tear it up!
Constant birth pangs. Frantic creation.
Slow down. Smoker's cough and eyes burning.
The book is rounding out. It's almost finished.
He feels full. He feels empty.
Has recurring premonitions of death
thirty years ahead of time. His vision blurs.
The book has grown much larger than he is.
Rain. Rain. Endless rain.
The dam breaks, flooding the migrants' camp,
engulfing the car of the composite family
who escape to a barn on higher ground
where Rose of Sharon, the composite daughter,
nurses the composite starving man.
It's finished! It's over! Now Steinbeck can die.
Now, in capital letters, it's THE END.

> *Thanks to Penguin USA for permission
> to use parts of John Steinbeck's diary,
> "Working Days."*

PAGANINI

Nicolo, so tall and haggard,
long black hair draped down to his shoulders,
dark cloak, fierce glare
and heavy mephistophelian brows.
This corny showman, this charlatan
would be lifted up through a hole in the stage,
then glide about in his spooky way
playing violin passages powerful enough
to hypnotize everyone there.

Driven by his tyrannical father
who forced him to practice, practice, practice
and taught him gambling and show business tricks.
Before he was seven he outplayed his teacher,
gave his first public concert when he was nine,
a great technician, a virtuoso,
a violin master of tone and touch.
Deep feeling honed to a fine art.
Technique no one thought humanly possible.

No, he didn't strangle the princess he lived with
in her cozy castle in Tuscany.
Didn't even kill his own mother
and wasn't tossed in a filthy dungeon
with the violin he played like a madman
until it had only one string left.
But it made good press and drew large crowds
who would swear that the devil stood by his side
manipulating his long bony fingers.
He could imitate birds with his violin,
draw lovers together or drive them apart
and could easily have lured the rats out of Hamlin.

His music brought him money and women
that his weakness for gambling syphoned away.
Made Director of Music by Napoleon's sister

and begat a son by a famous dancer.
But who would believe that he lived like a miser?
Painfully thin and always so cold
he kept bundled up, even in summer.

He died when he failed to obtain a license
to open his lavish gambling casino
But even his dying had frustrating problems
since none of the churches would bury a devil
who might rise up at night with his mad violin
to arouse base instincts, torment the dead
and desecrate the hallowed ground.
But remaining unburied became such an issue
that the Pope, far outranking any devil,
said, "Bury the man and be done with it!"
Yet even now, some who pass his grave
feel safer if they cross themselves.

CEZANNE

In the fields. . .in the house. . .even out in the rain
he kept painting, painting,
a tree or a rock or fruit on the table,
applying more color for light or shade.
Either got it right or tossed it away
out the window or down in the well
or sailed it off to the tall grass.
Driven by the urge to create
but year after year, for nineteen years,
rejected by the official salon,
the one indication of public acceptance.
The Salon wanted inoffensive paintings,
children playing. . .peaceful houses. . .
mother and child. . .discrete nudes.

He grew more irrational every year,
acting sullen or taken for mad.
Ignored or laughed at and never encouraged,
the butt of all jokes by critics and friends.
Not even the Exhibition of Losers
would allow him a square foot or two of their walls.
Grew long hair and a scraggly beard,
wore a tattered coat all spattered with paint.
A cause for comment wherever he went.

Rejection was something he grew to expect
but never be changed by. . .never give in to.
Each time a close friend laughed at his painting,
doubting him and the path he was taking,
he was driven farther into his head.
Worse losing a friend who misunderstood
than losing a friend by death.

Then, during the last ten years of his life,
his direction unchanged but his beard neatly trimmed
and he'd made some sort of peace with himself,
a Paris art dealer named Vollard
traveled to Aix where Cezanne was living.
He bought up every painting he could,
causing local peasants to comb their fields
for paintings Cezanne had thrown away,
removing them from the cracks in their walls
and looking for them in piles of trash
to sell to the rich fool who came there to buy
the works of the poor fool who painted them.

All the artists of Paris suddenly changed
from derision and laughter to earnest disciples
of this great impressionist, Cezanne.
His unorthodox method of painting a picture
was no longer sloppy, but true art.
And the critics changed. And the public changed.
And Cezanne, who died from painting the rain
may be smiling, finally that he was right.

THE TROUBADOUR CHRONICLES

When half the world was still in haze
there was a land of tumblers and jugglers,
singers and clowns, somewhere in the vines of France,
men of harp and mandolin, gaudy shirts and pantaloons
followed along their sunny ways by tawny women
full in the brisket and clear in the voice
who, hearing a drum or a wild song,
would unfurl their skirts in twirling dancing,
they and their dogs and their flower-faced children
all walking through fat green fields
or wandering through tunnels of linden and ash
or singing down trails of glassy lakes.

Sang for their meals in fortified castles,
dulcimer songs in three-part inventions
of heroes and wizards and dragons and love,
tossed roses to ladies in linen and laces,
shook tambourines for kings and queens,
told jokes to put smiles on their playing-card faces,
plink and pluck and tootle and laugh
leaving everyone drunk without drinking.

But Saracens living by tooth and claw
and Goths and Anti-Goths and Huns
despised the Troubadours and their tambourine songs.
Burgundians born with knives in their eyes
resented them and their grasshopper ways
and blamed them for every imbecile born.
Finally, in armor and helmets of steel
and mounted on horses that breathed out flame
they charged with scimitar and lance
slashing and clubbing the Troubadours
like so many hogs or captured things,
killing the men and the sound of their music
and whisking away their daughters and wives
who hadn't yet thrown themselves into the sea.

Harps in the willows hung there in sorrow
by women whose eyes were boarded-up windows
on that day of the locust, of crones spitting curses
and golden braids hanging down from the towers.
Now little remains of those musical people.
Part of a tune or the twist of a dance
has survived through ages of chromosomes;
or in towns of dull houses and sausage men
who brandish their pigs-feet-and-cabbage ideals
there might be a boy, or maybe a girl,
who sings a song of preposterous words
while skipping down paths of blue and red birds
under all the shades of sky.

QUEEN CHRISTINA

Greta Garbo, gangly in her shoes,
wrapped in fog as she strolled the deck
until, in a matter of days, she landed where
a midnight sun of flashbulbs stripped away
her gray and heavy echoes of Sweden.

During the season when birds come,
when lovers walk through fields of mint
or dally in their tubs,
the cameras fed on her face and nibbled at her eyes.

But during those years when money changed to guns
and the boots marched and the blood bled
she faded with each picture, each frame of film,
growing gradually transparent and Scandinavian wan,
asking to be alone.
Since she was neither Bronx nor Middlewest
she was cast as Russian, French, or anything
but always the camera draining her emotions,

even as Camille coughing her lungs out
or as the Bolshevik trying not to smile
or as the incognito Swedish Queen
after her country tavern love,
touching the bedroom furniture goodbye.

Finally, in New York,
where church bells ring through financial streets
and the rain she walks in has a lonely taste,
the cameras await each wrinkle of her face,
slowly photographing her away.

ART GALLERY

Nude Beneath the Willows, leaves hanging down.
Nude Descending Staircase, beige and brown.
Nude in an Armchair. Nude on a Train
Nude Bathers bathing in the summer rain.

Nude in the Forest. Nude in the Street.
Nude on the Sofa, lonely and discreet.
Nude Under pine Tree, bent out of shape
breast for an elbow and head like a grape.

Nude without bikini, tan here and there.
Nude in the Meadow drifting through the air.
Nude in the coffee shop glaring at me
wearing dress and raincoat that I can't see.

MATISSE

He began with still life,
a jar. . .a plant. . .the folds of fabric
and finally discovered women,
models chosen by love at first sight,
always interested in their lives,
in what they thought or talked about.
His brush in his hand, its bristles his fingers
feeling, appraising, loving, creating
like a sculptor or lover, a form of worship.

Just as King David sang his psalms,
Matisse painted women, his way of praising
over and over and over
until their lips became like the figure "three"
the eyes a slash or an oval coin
the nose a graceful, sweeping line,
the hand like a flower at the end of its stalk.
He knew how fabric lies against flesh,
how straps and ribbons cross and slip,
wind and flow by the waist or the armpit,
cross and curve beneath the breast
voluptuous, sensuous, lavish, lush.
Matisse, born old, born simple enough
to constantly praise.

The war with its indiscriminate death:
cities bombed, the downfall of France.
How should an artist express his time?
Or why should an artist express his time?
What had all this to do with his world
of Byzantine women in gold brocade,
women in armchairs, women at tables
reclining women of flute and guitar
or dreamy women of deep green jungle?

If you don't like your world, create one you do.
But he'd lived too long in his special world
impervious to either peace or war,
blazing flowers and cockatoos,
emerald serpents, radiant skirts,
bright colored flowers and cockatoos,
emerald serpents, radiant skirts,
women of pearls and precious stones
nude or draped or fully clothed,
Marguerite, Jacqueline, Yvonne and Loretta
bougainvillaea and towering palm,
Lydia, Sarah and princess Galitzine.
At eighty he felt he was in his prime
saying, All art worthy of being called art
is religious. A way of praising.
A way of life.

AT THE GRAVE OF MAXWELL BODENHEIM

He isn't there.
They've dug eight feet down with spades and trowels
pouring all the dirt through grading screens
and gathered up what fragments there were
to be brushed off and studied later,
but no Bodenheim.
Only rusty bolts and bottle caps,
nails and shards of coffee cups
and bits of what were thought to be bone
but proved to be some sort of antler.

Perhaps he'd had enough of earth
feeling Death at his heels as he moved through
the skid rows of his world. And all the while
his head boiling with words and their echoes,
"Beloved" meaning woman meaning touch meaning warm,

"Love" meaning life with its pulse throb. . .
its drumming rain. . .its trumpets of sunlight.
But all that poetry took flight
when he and his wife or whoever she was
were bludgeoned to death by a drunken sailor.
Since ascension has been proven possible
he must have gone with the sleeping birds
that were nesting in Death's frozen hair.

So go on, pay your respects.
Stand with your head bowed on the gravel path
by the grass where he's supposed to be.
Bring your flowers and stand with all those poets
who've made their Bodenheim pilgrimage.
But don't believe the inscription
on that rain-smoothed rock.
"Here lies" is a lie.
There are no bones of Bodenheim resting here.

THE MORTALITY OF STONE

Statues erode so slowly,
through nights and nights of owl cries
and days of stranded fish,
that strain to join buried fragments
of jugs and old bones
to attain the same disintegration
accorded the non-illustrious dead.

Buddha lying on his side in the jungle
veiled by giant leaves and tendril vines.
The angels of Venice
begin slowly worn away by eyes.
St. Francis lifting his severed hand in benediction.
And the emasculated Greek
forever running into the future
bearing his shattered marble flame.

And the heroes, the conquerors,
eaten away like gingerbread men.
Noseless Caesar with his fractured laurels.
Pallas Athena with her gradual mastectomy.
And Napoleon without his granite jaw
on a horse that has no face,
still riding through some cremated village,
what a victory of limbless trees
and lost cats mewing in the rubble.

And the armless warriors,
valiant without their swords.
The headless lovers caressing each other's stone.
Even Hercules, the quadruple amputee,
so pathetic with his residue of muscles.
All have lived through the same prosaic cycle —
unveiling, cheering, apathy, and pigeons —
everything but the final dissolution
that's needed if they expect to live again.

THE DAY GEORGE GERSHWIN DIED

The word, in voices of disbelief,
spread like an indelible stain
"George Gershwin is dead!"
Rolled across cities of snoring houses
and sidewalk cafes on the streets of Paris,
"Gershwin is dead! George Gershwin is dead!"
By radio waves that shook the world
or the sudden awareness of psychic women,
everyone heard that Gershwin was dead,
dead in his thirties like several good men,
Mozart, Jesus, or Vincent Van Gogh.
The organ grinders and penny arcades
still echoing memories of his songs,
"Summertime" and "I got Rhythm."

And Tin Pan Alley on 28th Street
hummed "Embraceable You" and "They All Laughed."
But no one sang. And no one smiled.

People are made in a strange way:
Gershwin was no one until he was ten,
heard shadows of music but paid no attention,
too busy with baseball, wrestling and hockey.
Provoker of fights, a petty thief,
cardplayer, and now and then billiards and pool.
Until the day of the magic wand,
the bow of an eight-year-old violinist
that stripped away his aimlessness
to reveal a new Gershwin obsessed with music,
who had to have lessons and have a piano,
had to play the piano. . .play the piano. . .
soaking up harmony, rhythm and counterpoint,
had to play the piano and write songs.

When he reached fifteen he became an adult,
quitting school to play songs in Tin Pan Alley.
Wrote Broadway musicals year after year,
usually with a cigar in his mouth,
each with songs that are gone by now
as though they'd been written on the wind,
each with songs that will live on forever,
part of the cosmos, part of our lives,
still being played wherever there's music
"Concerto in F," "Rhapsody In Blue,"
handed down through the ceiling
or dredged from his soul
"April In Paris" and "Strike Up The Band."

When his muse decided to rest for awhile,
he called it writer's block, turning to therapy.
Then later blacked out while leading an orchestra
and once gnawed a chair leg, like Nebuchadnezzar.
When they finally looked into his brain, he died.

HART CRANE

The few passengers on the ship
who lay in their deck chairs enjoying the sun
had no way of knowing the thoughts of this man
who so nervously strolled back and forth.
He felt the muse who had guided his pen
had abandoned him in her feminine way,
that his life, the world, and everything in it
was beginning to feel like standing barefoot
in a soggy, rain-drenched barnyard.
And the poems he conceived as a rare vintage
seemed to spill on the page like wine gone sour.
Better its grapes had been left on the vine.
Oh, the total result of all he had worked for
was slim pay indeed for the constant struggle.

But what a surprise to his deck chair audience
when he stood on the railing and dove in the ocean —
not gracefully, but effectively —
submerging, then bobbing up and down,
and swimming desperately, trying to catch up
with the ship that had been his springboard to death.

Not nearly as fortunate as Tchaikovsky
that night he decided the Neva River
was much too cold for drowning.
More like those who leap from their buildings,
then claw at the air on the way down
as though there were branches or hands to grab onto
when they invariably reconsider,
when they realize death is not for them.

MAGRITTE

Always hid who he really was,
artist in advertising,
fond of playing practical jokes.
Walked along the streets of Brussels
dressed like any normal man,
wearing the hat he might have been born with,
looking much like a banker or office manager,
his head full of numbers, all held in place
by the bowler hat that was part of him.
But who would surmise there were blue skies there
and a tuba and a comfortable chair
both in flames as they hung in the air
or even sense that this was Magritte,
his head buzzing with painting ideas.

Painted more napes of necks than mouths or eyes,
more backs of heads than faces
and even those were obscured by a haze
or an egg or an apple, or a bouquet of violets.
Some faces even wrapped with cloth,
a sign of his innate secrecy
or an echo, perhaps, of his mother found drowned,
her nightgown wrapped around her head.
Or because human faces are often distracting.

There's Magritte now, looking up at the moon.
You know it's him by the back of his head
and the bowler hat and the overcoat
and you hear him thinking: the function of painting
is to make the feeling of poetry visible,
furniture that appears to dream
and a torso or two as a constant reminder
that the world is endowed with mystery.

SHAKESPEARE

It was just as far to Stratford
as it was from life to death; but he left London
after there were no more plays in him.
Maybe he'd regain his health, though he forgot
that home was stray pigs that squealed by the windows,
neighbors, preferring dog-fights to poetry,
squealing down the road,
and his daughters noisy with their raucous voices.
He rode his horse to prove how young he was,
then limped from being tired and old.

Ghosts of duels, poison and intrigue
and crazy kings and murdered queens
kept spinning through his head,
royal courts of trumpets and roses,
and empires buried in the sand.
And he in love with women he'd created,
women who'd love him or betray him,
surrender or tease or smile or rage
or lead him gently by the hand
and slip stilettos in his heart as he slept,
perchance to dream, perchance to grow old,
as he had, reliving that residue
of nights alone, writing,
surrounded by his tavern friends or candlelight
as he injected life into those people of his plays.

Until the day Death hobbled through the valley
disguised as two old friends from London
who laughed with him as they'd always laughed,
talked and drank as they always had.
But this time he drank one glass too many
causing a certain vagueness in his head.
After they left as he walked off accompanied
by the background music of country noise
succumbing to the ultimate writer's block,
to rejoin his cast of characters at last.

A TALE OF TWO CITIES

Ronald Coleman,
all his life debauched and aimless,
stands clear-eyed and heroic
bound for the guillotine
in this, his finest hour.

White shirt open at the throat
he comforts the frightened, trusting blonde
as they ride together in the rocking tumbrel
through screaming streets of sewer stink
and raw tobacco spittle,
inching past the legless beggar
past the old vindictive bitch who watches
shaking her ruins with loony laughter.
Then, from that carnival of popcorn, hamburgers and beer
comes the jeering and cries of the cloven-hoofed crowd
demanding his head on a platter
demanding tomato blood and giblet soup
screaming for the surprising yellow root of his being.

It is there in the sweet iambics of the afternoon
that Ronald Coleman, unbuttoner of dresses,
loosener of tresses,
dreamer. . .drinker of burgundy. . .
ascends the platform steps.
The guillotine is a shadow of its timbers.
And the lethal blade,
the basket for the noble heads,
the authorities so be-business-suited stern.
Even the executioner a man of hat, cravat and gloves
while Ronald Coleman, doomed but human,
looks up at the tumbling cotton clouds
looks down at the cobblestone people
looks far off at the rubber hills
beyond the fields of yesterday.

And it's then, in this best of times
in this worst of times,
that he acts out his paltry destiny
of choosing death to marriage,
rambling on like some converted drunk
about this is the best thing he has ever done,
kneeling at last before the preposterous guillotine
that breaks him down to basic chemicals
and frees him from the tumult of his mind
while gradually a choir of sound-track voices
blends him with a breeze.

THE GARDEN OF LOVE

Peter Paul Rubens, his brush an extension of desire,
his head packed with battles and biblical stories
and family and color and broad-brimmed hats,
mythological beings as he felt they should look..

His paintings so vigorously brushed
full with moving, acting, working people,
that Contemplation gave up and left
muttering and mumbling "All that flesh!"
or, "Heroines built like cleaning women!"
Painted men who resembled Samson or Hercules,
women as graceful, zaftig nudes
still being referred to as Rubenesque.
A great connoisseur of buttocks and breasts
and, to be fair, of faces and hands.
Adam and Eve and The last Judgment
a superabundance of movement and power.

When his first wife was buried
and he fifty-three with ten years to go,

he married a sister of one of her in-laws,
sixteen-year-old Helena Fourment
who matched his mental model of women.
Her features had often appeared in his paintings
before he had known her, before she was
born...Venus, Mary Magdalene and Madonna...
a strange case of Art's effect on Nature.
Helena in furs. Helena as Venus.
Helena his wife in The Garden Of Love
crowded with in-laws and jubilant neighbors
with bare-assed cherubs flying over them all.

That golden decade, his culmination,
cathedral ceilings and altar pieces,
saints and apostles and holy men
with strong, driven Biblical faces,
each a celebration of life.
Painted robust and raucous Flemish peasants
with their Rabelaisian zest for living
talking and laughing and nursing infants
or drinking or drunk or making love.

Peter Paul Rubens, worn away
by his palette and brush and hunger for life
as Helena, his idol and inspiration,
gave him youth and old age at the same time,
gave him four healthy children he used as models
and a fifth born eight months after he died.

CHAGALL

Born in a little Russian village
where all the houses were topsy-turvy.
Even the heads of some of the people
were upside down or completely detached.
Born with an urge to praise God

by painting everything he saw,
even dragging his childhood through life
and painting it over and over and over
with a mixture of color and homesick tears
the horse and wagon in the air
drifting past his open window
as a fiddler sits on the neighbor's chimney
putting the day to music.

Lovers in green. . .lovers in blue. . .
lovers with wrinkles, their years on their faces.
Lovers on a donkey's back
or the moon a crescent in the sky
as the lovers float above the town,
as a bridesmaid drifts in through the window.
"Art," he said, "is a state of mind."

The Bible so much a part of his life
he thought Jacob and Isaac lived down the road
and he wouldn't have been a bit surprised
if Goliath came looming over the hill.

His village of animals and people,
all sharing the same sad ending.
Talk to the cow. . .confide in the cow. . .
on cold mornings milking the steaming cow. . .
watching his grandfather slaughter the cow. . .
refusing, but finally eating the cow,
then forever the cow being part of him.

Chagall. . .Chagall. . .I saw him once
as he watched the workmen build his mosaic
by the Dearborn side of the First National Bank.
Maybe he saw me. Maybe not.
Maybe he even painted my picture
wearing my suit and a horse's head.
Or maybe floating slightly above him
looking down on him
smiling my blessing.

REMBRANDT

Rembrandt, so in love with his wife,
bouncing her on his lap at their wedding
and she wondering, "What next?"
Holding his glass of wine in the air,
his dapper moustache, his smart Alec smile.
You'd cringe if the bride were your daughter.

Painted her in jewelry and cloaks.
Painted her in sunlight and shadow.
Painted her velvet and painted her nude,
on paper used for wrapping fish
or wadded up to plug chinks in the walls.
Made love to her in word and deed,
two daughters who lived for just part of a day.
a son who lived a month or two,
He painted Girl at the Half Door
and Woman Bathing Her Feet in the Brook.

But his son Titus, Titus lived!
Titus lived but his mother died
leaving Rembrandt alone with a son
who smiled like an angel and spit up blood,
blood on his pillow. . .blood on his cup.
Death like a halo, kept hovering
while Rembrandt painted The Night Watch,
and painted An Old Lady With a Book,
An Old Woman Cutting Her Nails.

Titus, when he was old enough,
married Magdalena Van Loo
who felt she could have married better.
She enticed him with her loveless flesh,
her trite breasts, her wrestler's thighs
and soon stood mourning, dressed in black,
hard-faced praying mantis.

When Titus died and returned to heaven,
Rembrandt painted The Prodigal Son
Then placed a mirror beside his easel
to paint himself, the lone survivor.
Painted the lines of his strong face
drawn by each of his lost loves.
He painted his eyes filled with memories.
Painted the end of his life.

REMBRANDT'S SON

And so Titus married Magdalena,
well endowed physically but disagreeable
while he inherited his mother's frail lungs
and his father's compulsion to create.

But not with colors for him to carefully blend
and apply to mountains of empty canvas
so he could paint his wife in robes and veils
and crowns as Rembrandt had with Saskia.

Instead, since talent had been withheld from him,
he set about creating in the only way he could —
snuffed out the candles early each evening and,
clinging to his wife as a barnacle to a ship,
hammered out the daughter he'd never live to see.

SHERWOOD ANDERSON

He'd work at whatever Ohio had to offer—
livery stable or bicycle builder,
paint factory or copy writer,
dreaming of cars and country clubs
and the wealth he was almost certain to have
as long as he kept on working...working,
Even a business of his own.
His vacation — the Spanish American War.

But unaware of the stories in him,
unaware that every face he saw
each house he entered, workers he worked with,
the nuances of voices he heard,
women's eyes and legs and smiles
and every morsel of small town gossip
were all like seeds being sown in him
that would gradually mature and ripen
to almost bursting, ready to pick.

Until one night of no sleep
when the madness took over and harvest began,
condemning him to a lifetime of scribbling
words that kept flowing from his pen
to tear him away from his business and marriage,
reducing him to rented rooms —
first in Cleveland, then in Chicago.

As a sculptor needs a model to go by,
he kept adding living to his living —
drinking, carousing, studying others,
eavesdropping and Peeping-Toming
or spending hours in restaurants talking
with friends like Ben Hecht and Bodenheim,
talking of words and writers and writing —
not what to write but what not to write.

His scribbling, scribbling, constant scribbling
had distilled his life to a group of stories
in which he was George and his hometown Winesburg
and explaining, at last, what lay beyond
the faraway look in his eyes.
True stories...conjured-up stories
of men he had worked with, the goals they aimed for
and how success or failure had changed them.
Or of women in business or down the hall
and their ways of handling loneliness.
each story close to the raw nerves
of a country still only halfway between
puritan pilgrims and now.

His Winesburg, Ohio drove old friends away
just as it drew some new friends close.
Yet, when he reached the end of his memoirs
he reached the compensating conclusion
that his had been a most wonderful life.

THE NOVELIST

I have the urge to write a Russian novel,
live it, breathe it, slowly becoming Russian
until I'm finished being young Mikhail
or beautiful Natasha so in love with him,
finished being a hundred thousand others
from serf to prince, chambermaid to queen.

This Natasha, she so tender in her years,
sitting at her mirror while Maryushka and Svetlana
dab her cheeks with powder and arrange her hair
for the Grand Ball in the palace.
I make her and young Mikhail radiant dancers

whirling, gliding, half in heaven, half in dream
as they float across the floor so unaware,
like everyone, that within a week her young Mikhail,
his eyes glazed over, would be lying on a battle field
gazing sightless at the clouds.
All the dancers, Count Baronski, the seated chaperones
and even me completely shaken by the news.

Ah, Natasha, how she wept, so overcome with grief
and the horror of seeing decades stretch before her
sprinkled with unsavory men with thick, caressless hands:
Vladimir Basilikov and Boris Kalgorin. Eyes of passion.
Brows of hate. Men who made her fingers flutter up
helplessly to protect her throat.
Natasha, so completely Russian, as the Volga,
as the mountains, as the very soil she stood on
but so devastated by this shattering bereavement.

If only I could somehow brighten up her future,
but how could I intrude and change her destiny?
A writer must be faithful to his craft,
trust the scribbled words the karandash reveals.
But soon I grow so numbed by tragedy no tears are left,
no longer have the appropriate response
for Natasha's dismal circumstances.
Even become allergic to her frequent tears.

So finally, spurning my writer's Hippocratic oath
to follow where the pencil leads, I tear up chapters
four through nine and return to the Grand Ball
to watch Natasha and Mikhail dance,
together once again, enchanted by each other.
I decide to have him be a government food inspector,
then ramble on through chapter after chapter
guarding their cyrillic lives, watching their children grow
and making sure they always stay in love.

PETER BRUEGEL — (1525-1569)

The world had grown used to paintings from Italy —
warm skies and delicate women,
their faces kissed by the Mediterranean.
Not the hard, cold Netherlands skies
that Bruegel knew so well and painted,
nor the sturdy madonnas and buxom brides
and the hunched-over, plodding peasants,
their minds as gnarled as their hands.

His religious paintings, all set in his homeland
seemed so Nordic...so unbiblical.
Those lumpy figures — nothing like Galilee
where people wore robes and pious faces.
One of these paintings — "Carrying the Cross,"
seemed like a vacation — a carnival
with horses prancing and children running
and crowds of Dutch peasants waiting to see
Christ nailed to the cross on a local hill —
painted as Bruegel felt it should be.

He painted crowds listening to wild John the Baptist
or looking on as St. Paul was struck blind,
painted people in the snow-covered village
as government soldiers slaughtered their children —
footprints and hoofprints and blood on the snow.
Since the Spanish rulers were over-religious
and considered non-Catholics "the enemy,"
Bruegel painted the villagers watching
as though they were thinking of something else
and really didn't care.

Much safer to paint an everyday face
than reveal any sign of dissent
as children and friends were being stabbed
by the Spanish Inquisition machine.
Yet he managed to separate caution from Art
because Art, like every living thing,
depends on the breath of life to survive.

THE PAINTER

He begins with a dab of blue
and the council members mumble their approval,
because he has begun the great mural.

Then he adds some yellow, and some grey,
and soon they can see a bird take shape.
And they discuss this first symbolic figure
in the mural of their city.

Then he paints patches of cloud, and some sky,
more blue sky, more blue-grey sky,
more sighing and infinite sky,
and he adds some mossy green and pungent brown
and soon they can see a claw of the tree,
and slowly the loins and shoulders and crotch of the tree.
And he has the tree rooted to the earth,
to the vast landscape of earth that spreads
far, far across his huge mural.

The bird and the sky and the tree and the earth.

And he brushes in real figures of men and women
walking along a road that leads to the vanishing point,
the men large and strong and glad,
wearing crimsom and teal plumes in their hats
and singing roundly and playing guitars,
and the women with strong brown legs
carrying baskets of plump and ripened fruit and ringing bells
and some with white doves perched on their shoulders.
And there are children strewing flowers along the way.
He paints a waterfall draped over the side of a hill
and bright balloons of prayer rising up to the sky.

But they say this is not their city.
Where are the drawn shades and the furtive eyes
and the blood oozing from under the doors?
Where is the filth and the fear and the furious sky?

Where is the violence and the death?
And the rats. Where are the rats?
How could anyone call this a painting of their city?
They relieve him of his commission
and revile him and malign him
and set the dogs on him to drive him away.

So he gathers up his brushes and paint
and walks off along the streets of the city
followed by large strong men
who wear plumes in their hats
and sing and play guitars,
and by women with strong brown legs
who carry baskets of fruit and ring bells
or have white doves perched on their shoulders,
and by children who strew flowers along the way.
And wherever they go bright balloons of prayer
rise up to the sky.

SUBJECT MATTER

All these grassy pools and cut flowers
and fruit on the table, and fish. . .
Sometime I'd like to paint Juanita,
her frightened eyes. . .her calm classic eyes.
Oil on canvas, or maybe acrylic.
Maybe wearing a bracelet or rings,
but nothing else — just her.
Maybe holding a cluster of grapes. . .or a glass,
her head tossed back — big bacchanalian scene
with cloven-hoofed piper in the background
or old pot-bellied lush with grapes for a beard
ogling her with drunken fascination.

Or maybe some desolate, almost midnight backdrop,
everything floating about in the eye of a storm
or a Witches' Sabbath on top of Bald Mountain —
hawks with serpents in their beaks,
leafless trees reaching out to her,
she wearing a crown of precious stones.
Maybe add some white for contrast —
a lamb in its meadow, or a long-haired cat.

But Juanita wouldn't do it. Much too skittish,
rather slip some tasteful picture of her
under the door, expecting me to work from that
September Morn of her with scarves
or wearing a pristine little tutu
left over from her school dance recital.

Or worse — show up with her sad-faced family
protecting their closely guarded daughter,
big pillowy mother, scraggly migrant father
and little brothers muttering their native tongue,
all standing like they were just off the boat
while I try to recapture the groove of her lip
and the curve of her earlobes near the neck
or erasing the moss beneath her arms
and changing those first bold schemes
with leotards and veils.

Maybe Mrs. Kraus would be the best model,
she with those ex-lovers sunk in her heart.
She's sprung her lines with beer and cabbage
and cracks her knuckles now and then.
But I see her in a blue skirt and topless,
defending the barricades of Paris.

DIANE ARBUS

Mommy and Daddy and governess,
she left all that for love and a marriage
that left her at last with two young daughters
and a camera virus that ravaged her life,
left her searching The Bronx and The Village
for faces to click, for masks to remove,
a Rolleiflex dangling from her neck
to protect her on the dingy streets,
like a rabbits foot, or The Ruby Slippers.

Lived in a loft, in a made-over stable,
and shy. Barely able to ask for assignments
but Click! Click! A hundred clicks. . .
often more to reveal a soul or a feeling,
to reveal the shape of daydreams or nightmares,
like finding strange thoughts in a friend's face.
Fighting the camera, often forgetting to realize
it's not what she wants but what it wants
with its irony and fantasy built in.
Staring sensitive midgets in the eye.
Going nude to photograph overweight nudists.
Clicking burlesque shows, the flabby strippers
relaxed in their stagnant dressing rooms.
And pinheads and geeks and the man who ate lightbulbs.

Photographing a face is an act of unveiling,
laying bare carefully hidden feelings
no one had ever suspected before,
capturing suicide in the eyes,
revealing guilt, revealing love,
because it's all there! Everything's there!
The parents amazed at life in their child,
the child unaware that it sprang from its parents.
But the best pictures come when one is afraid:
clicking her father dying of cancer,
or trailing a stranger through dark shabby halls

or a transvestite uneasy in his room.
Then the public show: The Exhibition
every morning wiping spit from her pictures.

But some sort of haze in her mother's blood
made her subject to cavernous bouts of depression.
Curled up in a corner. Curled up on the roof.
Spent over a week brooding over a picture
but no longer nourished by her camera.
The camera is sinister, so mysterious.
It can actually capture a person's soul.
She telephoned everyone, talked and talked
frantic with things she had to say
until they discovered her in her tub
severed from all she could not understand.

*— With thanks to Patricia Bosworth's
biography, "Diane Arbus"*

MODIGLIANI

On the morning when memory began
he, painter of flowers
and bowls of fruit
and slender faces,
sat in his usual restaurant
huddled in his three sweaters,
harboring his weak lungs,
frail in his thin blood,
hoarding the warmth of his ritual coffee.

Then this girl, this Galatea,
locked in a pocket of sun near the window,
bathed in fire, in the world's first light,
and he like Adam, testing his limbs,

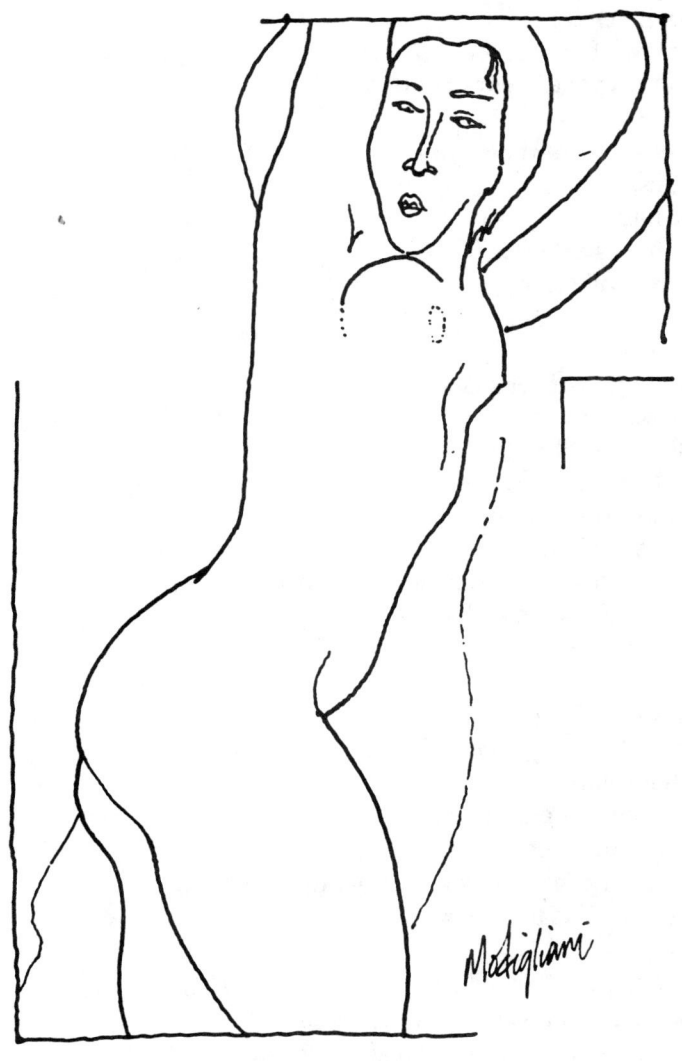

slowly, painfully, sketching her face,
the line of her nose,
the shadow of her cheek,
the incipient valley below her throat.

He dressed her in white robes,
in turbans,
in large hats,
painted her as a dancer,
as the prow of a ship,
as a tree,
as a flame
painted jungles of her shadow
and landscapes of her thighs,
painted her as she slept,
as leaf shadows flecked her skin like tears,
as she was prim,
as she was wild.
The walls of his rooms were murals of her,
the tunnels of his brain alive with her,
he who sipped life like a weak tea.

But she was a fierce wind
that turned his compulsion to frenzy,
a scorching sun
that gave him the glow of death
until all he could see were her eyes
looking down at him like the memory of smoke,
far above him like two vague planets.

When his fingers stopped tracing her face in the air,
when her life as a goddess came to an end
and the rooms of her Eden regained their squalor,
she turned away from his painted ikons
and flew from the window like a bird.

JAMES ENSOR

Born long before either you or I
in Ostend on the seacoast of Belgium
and on Friday the thirteenth, of all days.
A sea gull crashed onto his crib one night,
infecting him with a long-lasting terror.
At thirteen he began painting pictures
that teetered between reality
and the depths of his livid imagination.

In art school his avalanches of color
were greeted with cat-calls, jeering and punches,
a hint of the total rejection to come.
Their paintings were dark, but his were alive –
forerunners of Expressionism.
Just for the fun of using bright colors
he painted masks on some of his subjects –
ridiculous, outrageously comic masks, saying
"People try to hide what they're thinking."

James Ensor in a world of his own
painted "A Woman Eating Oysters,"
"Christ Being Mocked," and "Children Dressing."
Foolish paintings. Foolish painter.
He painted "Skeletons Trying To Keep Warm,"
and "The Entry Of Christ Into Brussels."
Rejected...Rejected...Always rejected.
He could hear the sound of the sea gull's wings.

In time the rejection and disapproval
had its effect until, when he was thirty-three ,
his obsession with painting was snuffed out.
His ideas fled, his genius waned
and what paintings he painted were repetitions.
He became a recluse, became alcoholic
and slowly his house became a museum

that guarded the fruits of his disappeared genius.
Long walks every evening to the Falstaff tavern
for his pints of beer and cheddar cheese bits.

The indefinable magic of music
was the only cure for his isolation.
He would play the harmonium to relax..
At seventy he gained his deserved recognition
when the King of Belgium declared him a baron
and slowly his name was resurrected.
Twenty years later, the sea gull's wings
flapped wilder than ever and carried him off,
over the hills and far away.

EDGAR DEGAS

He was put on earth to paint women —
women bathing or ironing clothes,
washing, drying, or combing their hair,
women dancing, bending and swaying,
always unaware of being watched
as though they were being seen through a keyhole.
And faces — painted faces beyond the surface
exposing their most intimate secrets.

Thought of himself as an independent,
a realist in every sense of the word,
subject matter and technique.
But certainly not an impressionist;
not the sort to be pigeonholed.

He and much younger Toulouse-Lautrec
were two of a kind — race tracks and music halls,
bawdy houses and dancing girls
and no love for Nature, the Great Outdoors.
The mountains he painted were barren hills,

trees and their foliage were blurs of green.
Even rows of his houses seemed melted together.

Edgar Degas married to his painting.
His models were beauties he kept at a distance
as though they were strangers fresh from Mars,
fascinating, but too distracting,
potentially dangerous, highly suspicious.
Only the dowdy and unattractive
could ever expect to become his housekeeper.
Like Walt Whitman, he might often have said,
"'til arise my aforefelt wonder of women."

He spent his life studying ballet dancers,
often only their flared skirts,
how they would bend, how they would sway.
When he grew old and could barely see
he still painted dancing girls. . .dancing girls,
their billowing skirts a flood stage of color
that spilled onto their arms and legs.
They're still locked in their dancing positions
and for all we know he's still up there painting
or dancing some vague dance.

WILHELM FRIEDEMANN BACH

Christian and Christoff, Gottfried and Carl,
Johann Sebastian's musical sons,
all composers and fine technicians.
And Friedemann, the oldest, the most gifted,
most closely approaching the old man's genius,
concertos, cantatas, fantasies, fugues.
Even thought in chords and musical phrases.
Yet he was the one who died broke,
the one most laughed at in local taverns,

dissipated and dissolute.
Great talent, but usually out of work.

Childhood had been the prime of his life,
curled up in the nest of his family
with music and talk, music and music,
tootle, tootle, plink and pluck
in that house full of children and relatives.
And always so anxious to please his father
who would take him on trips to hear "pretty tunes,"
who would laugh and clap when Friedemann played —
ho, ho! Big-bellied Bach.
But when he was ten he was cut in half
by grief over his mother's dying,
a bereavement that gnawed at the rest of his life.

The half that remained was his father, Sebastian,
that fountain of music he tried to surpass,
that foot-tapping orchestra puppeteer
who brought strings, brass and woodwinds to life,
urging music from each of the instruments —
huff, puff, laugh and shout,
swearing or nodding at violins,
warning the trumpets with one raised finger.
Even adding his voice to fortissimo parts.
And impatient — he once hurled his wig at the organist.
How grand to have such a father as he.

When old Bach died, his sons agreed
that Friedemann could easily take his place.
But with no one left he cared to impress
he was like a bundle of sticks on the shelf.
He'd inherited just as much temper as talent
so never found work that amounted to much —
church organist in a small German town
with a quiet river winding through it,
peaceful streets and sleepy houses
while cyclones of music raged through his head.

LEONARDO DA VINCI

Other people had souls that might fly off to heaven
or, if they deserved it, roast in Hell.
But he designed wings of eagle feathers
that he could strap onto his shoulders and fly,
soar aloft from the highest cliffs
with no special destination in mind.
At least it worked rather well on paper.
His soul, if he had one, was fireproof,
most likely shaped like a question mark
to nag his constantly probing mind
with "Why this?" or "Why that?" or "Why is it so?"

In Milan, the city of hangmen and vultures,
he wrote to the Duke applying for work:
"I can make catapults, mortars and cannon,
chariots with whirling knives on their wheels
and endless other means of offense,
firebombs with enough sulphur added
to stupefy their victims.
Or a bomb, when discharged in a walled-in courtyard,
that will heave up the roofs and shake the walls
as though a great earthquake were taking place.
I can make bombs that despise life,
causing miscarriages in women
or killing young chicks still in their shells."

This is the man who painted flowers,
painted studies of cats and dancing muses,
Madonna and Child with Saint Anne,
flowering rushes and Young John The Baptist.
He would study a mob in the throes of its riot
drawing various facial expressions,
but not much caring what made them upset.
Leonardo da Vinci, either Jekyl and Hyde
or completely absorbed by all of life.

FRANZ LISZT

First big concert when he was twelve.
A handsome child, rather frail and thin.
But those eyes," said the wise Hungarian women,
"think of all the hearts he'll break."
As though they'd foreseen Marie, the Comtesse
who bore him three children.
Or George Sand, the gadabout novelist,
so enchanted by him she bore him three children.

He was so adept at seducing an audience
he could make any disenchanted wife
sitting next to her oaf of a husband
grow misty over a long-dead love,
tremble to feel he was somewhere near
speaking to her in his intimate voice.
Even Chopin wished he could play his own etudes
the way Franz Liszt was able to play them.

How the women swooned and cried.
One salvaged the dregs of his tea as a keepsake,
one kept his cigar butt safe in her bosom.
They would take his gloves or cut shreds from his clothes
causing their men to grow puzzled and wonder
just what it was that drove them so wild.
The long hair? The high forehead?
Maybe standing the way Napoleon stood,
hand over his heart and deep in his coat.

But it was "the touch" they had come to hear,
feel him turn the opera house into a church.
And what a festival after the concert...
his wild admierers unhitching his horses
and dragging the coach back to his hotel
where Liszt would stand on his balcony
to hear his fans giving speeches and cheers.
Women would leave their families for him,

trade their insensitive scarecrow husbands
for the meaning of life only he could give,
this Hungarian with the faraway eyes
so lost in his world of tone poems and rhapsodies.
An insufferable man, as often as not,
lover and worshiper of women
like Carolyn, Charlotte, and Lola Montez,
but puzzled by words like "fidelity."

He spent the last third of his life in the church
camouflaged by his clerical cloak.
But still the women huddled around him
because no mater how he looked when he played,
they would recognize his touch.

THE POET IN THE CAGE

Sunny, sunny Italy had turned to guns and rain and mud;
now half the statues had arms blown off
and Mussolini hung upside down.
And Ezra Pound, for "siding with the enemy,"
was locked in a special welded cage,
scheduled for things like gallows and electric chairs.

Three weeks of the glaring sun of Pisa
and the dust and isolation of his cage
was all it took to nudge him as far off center
as the Leaning Tower itself,
weaving in and out of memory, judged too thin
and weak ever to stand trial for treason.
Was he playing possum?
Was he a chameleon, mad one day and sane the next,
hiding behind the veils of his mind?
Judged to be abnormal,
now suddenly undergoing further aberration,
Irrational, even for a poet.

Sang

喪⁴ 口₃₀ 衷₃₅₄ To lose, destroy, ruin, despond
|氣 ill-omened, down-hearted
|盡 to lose entirely
|父 lost his father
|良心 lose virtue or conscience
|命 to lose one's life 亡
|失 to lose, fail, e.g., |失自
|胆 afraid, disheartened

Sao

臊 膄 搔 騷 肉₁₃₀ 臊₆₃₇ 手₆₄ 馬₁₈₇ 蚤₇ₓ₇ Rancid, rank, tainted |的低
|氣 rank smell of fox, skunk
|肉 tainted meat
To scratch, irritate
|首 scratch the head
To stir up; sad, poetic
|擾 to harass, fidget
|人 a poet
勞| grieved, miserable

繅 掃 糸₁₂₀ 手₆₄ 巢₅₀₈ 帚₆₇₄ To reel off cocoons |絲
To sweep, clean up 打·|, ·|
|淨了 swept clean |乾淨
|除 to sweep away
|房 to clean house
|地 sweep ground or floor

嫂 女₃₈ 叟₆₈₁ Elder brother's wife, matron |·
|家 my elder brother's wife
|大 wife of eldest brother

槁 箒 手₆₄ 帚₆₇₄ A broom |帚
|興 bad fortune, dispirited
|星 a broom star—comet

噪 譟 口₃₀ 桌₆₃₇ Chirp of birds, hum of men
|蟬 chirping of cicadas

sao³

D
B

48

He took a room and stayed ten years
at St. Elizabeth's Asylum for the Insane,
comfy little place with desk and window bars
where he handled all his correspondence,
worked on his cantos and translations of Confucius,
won the Library of Congress prize for poetry
and received visitors, the leading poets of the day.

And always the cantos.
Always pouring himself into the cantos
as though each page were some well-formed amphora
preserving the distillation of his life.
The cantos. . .the cantos. . .
pulses of poetry mingled with a random mix
of languages and anecdotes and obscure histories,
fragments of the unusual, Chinese characters,
medieval madrigals, Egyptian hieroglyphs,
cantos of London and France, of Pisa and the Orient,
his entire life a journal of cryptic verses
requiring several keys to unlock it.

And when he was finished,
when his life of words, stopped flowing
he said,"I botched it all". Like a shop window,
I picked out all the things that caught my eye
and jumbled them in a bag.
But that's not the way to make a work of art."
Revealing, with that remark,
the cage he'd been locked up in all the time.

VASLAV NIJINSKY

The audience knew what ballet should be —
several young women in gauzy white costumes
bending and weaving, drifting and twirling
to almost soporific music —
music they'd heard...music they knew.
So the theater, its stage, their being there
was more like a reverie...more like a church,
a sort of prayer to blot out Europe
with its rattle of cannons, its simmering hates,
its marching armies, Kaiser and Tsar,
needing only a spark to explode the world —
maybe only one bullet for some little archduke.

Fluffy white women leaping and gliding
gave substance to their sterilized dreams,
but certainly no such revolting intrusion
as Nijinsky squeezing a cluster of grapes,
its juices all over his face and mouth.
Then, dressed in tights and a skin-tight top
all covered with spots to resemble some animal
crouching, playing his lascivious pipe,
then peeking through a barrier of leaves
at a group of nymphs approaching a pool.

One removes a part of her costume
to bathe, to casually shower herself
in a waterfall made of fluttering silks
causing "filthy, bestial, lecherous" Vaslav
to leap in the air, hang there for a moment
as though he knew nothing of gravity,
then drift down to land on his toes —
causing outbursts of booing and hissing
by an audience fearing the threat of change —
causing critics to wield and slash with their pencils:
"More animal than human..."
"More orgasm than dance..."

While Nijinsky, part chameleon
reflecting the animal costume he wore,
reflecting his time and the stage and his role,
danced as no one else could dance,
his hands and feet slowly winding and turning
or fluttering like a katydid's wing,
every movement precisely timed.
The nymphs he'd rehearsed to the edge of exhaustion
kept dancing through layers of color and music
like images of a dream.

Vaslav Nijinsky, his anonymous face
completely disguising his teeming brain
but later, when his mind closed down
and dancing on stage was out of the question
he relived his life in the diaries he kept
Petrushka...Firebird...Scheherazde...
Narcissus and the Rites of Spring,
signing himself, "God and Nijinsky."

HENRI DE TOULOUSE LAUTREC

He could have run the huge estate,
maybe doodling horses on ledger sheets.
Or hunted as his father had, drawing hounds
and foxes that race through the fields.
Could have lived for sparkling parties
sketching ladies in green and gold rooms,
their low-cut dresses and classic faces,
each model a potential friend.

But he fell and broke his legs instead,
to his father's disgust and his mother's sorrow.
He never grew taller after that,
the smallest of all their ancient line —
Toulouse Lautrec.

Toulouse Lautrec

Nothing to do after that but paint,
hide in his wine glass,
walk under the tables at Moulin Rouge
or between the legs of the women there —
sketching, drawing, painting and drinking.
Color economy. Minimal lines.
Painting Yvette and Jane and Marcelle,
the laundress and the English girl,
the girl with red hair and the bareback rider
and all their expressions and moods.

Drinking too much, painting too much —
top hats and derbies, cakewalks and waltzes,
the cancan girls and their stockings and petticoats.
Painting the bartender ruling Barry's,
painting orchestras and one-man bands.
Drunk with his colors. Drunk with his wine.

And then the unfurnished room with the view
of bleakness beyond the asylum windows.
Painting a long-ago circus from memory
then leaving by walking under the doors
to paint too much and drink too much
till his mother held him, as mothers do,
and he died in her arms, immortal.

VINCENT VAN GOGH

Swallows sweeping the sky are surprising.
Meadowlarks perched by paths through the prairie
or churches discovered on hidden roads,
the angels above them disguised as birds.
So it must have been for nine twisted years
to discover this almost laughable man
obsessed with painting the world as he saw it,
peasants digging. . .peasants gleaning. . .rough faces,
hands and feet, over and over and over.

With not enough money to pay for a model
he painted boats and rivers and trees,
fields of wheat and orchards in bloom,
red, blue, orange and green.
"Oh the beautiful tones that rain gives the soil."
Painted his bed and a chair and a table,
fish on a plate and flowers in a jar.
But who would buy paintings from such a fool?
He even painted over his paintings.
He even threw scores of his paintings away.

Three or four times he had failed at love.
What woman would share such contagious unrest
or find comfort near the glare of his eyes?
He painted the stars and the blinding sun,
Chrome Yellow. . .Prussian Blue. . .
violent trees and violent skies,
Burnt Umber and Malachite.
Driven mad by the roaring wind
that jostled his arm and ran off with his easel.

But "Success" and "Failure" were foreign words.
"I see the way before me clearly."
His brush flicked with the speed of light,
his blended color, an inspiration.
And when he felt he had conquered himself

was it madness to cut off part of his ear?
Or was it symbolic when he, like a matador,
gave it to the fairest of women,
a barmaid in the local pub?
More and more he painted the Sun
all shades of yellow, the color of madness.
"My future's the cup from which I must drink."
Painted a church and crows in a field,
then borrowed a pistol and shot himself
and died in his sleep a day or two later
leaving his paintings for people to say,
That's how a tree should look!
and Look at the pond and the tired old horse!
and See the Sun! and Look at the stars!
seeing all they had known for the first time ever.

DALI AND VAN GOGH

It seemed so important to Senora Dali
to have a son named for her husband
that she buried her dead son Salvador
and named her new son, Salvador,
causing that name to ring through his blood
like echoes in a cave.
Barely knowing who he really was,
he painted in his corner of haunted Spain
living in the shadow of his brother,
straining to surpass the genius
of that buried and much-loved "Real Salvador."

And Frau Van Gogh, determined to produce
a son to carry on his uncle's name,
replaced her dead son Vincent with another Vincent
who walked past little Vincent's grave so often
that soon its spirit mingled with his own,
and drove him from Holland to painting and madness.

Perhaps those doubts of who he was caused Salvador
to greet his one love with a flower behind his ear,
armpits shaved down to the blood, and his body
smeared with goat's dung mixed with laundry bluing.
While Vincent, reacting just about the same
toward a waitress who had smiled at him.
He suddenly became both matador and bull
and, standing victorious over his own defeated self,
cut off his ear and offered it to her.

Since Salvador's absurdities were tenderly received
he lived a life of love, painting soft pianos,
liquid watches, resurrections, fish and crutches,
with intricate technique, his moustache, brush and art
surreal and meticulously trained. But Vincent,
whose gift provoked a panic of disgust,
flung his brush through fields of angry wheat,
painting nights of stars spinning from their orbits
and violent trees that flailed the air
until the fire that drove him burned so strong
he finally found a gun and blew it out.

EDWIN GRAUER PAINTING THE BATTLE OF SAN MICHELE

The canvas is 31½ by 47 inches.
He draws the horizon
and then he paints a tumbling sky
with clouds heavy as udders aching to be milked.
And under the horizon, the sea,
its surface slow to anger, but rapidly growing dark.
He paints the castle of San Michele on the faraway shore —
blurred in a haze..sky draped over its towers.
And he has liquid trees flowing across the hills.
Their leaves seem tired of summer.

But it is the large meadow that is most important.
The action will center here.
It is sliced by a narrow creek
that will soon be warm with blood.
In the left side the uniforms will be a light khaki,
to the right they will be somewhat darker — almost grey.
Other than that the soldiers will look the same.

There will be hand-to-hand combat..fixed bayonets..
all in the pervading muck churned up from the creek.
Shattered bodies will lie sprawled on the grass.
He will paint the screams of the ruined faces
and the disembowelled horses.
The dead will achieve a colorless anonymity
as a vapor of life escapes from the bodies.
Even some birds will be killed,
and several trees.

But Grauer's soldiers are not made for war.
He sketches their heads on scratch paper,
practices drawing their movements,
but it's useless.
Each one seems too much like him,
has his delicate hands and thoughtful face.
Each one moves in a gangling way.
It is impossible for him to paint stone in their faces
or ferocity in the hooves of their horses.
Their eyes are dreaming of something else
and there is nothing he can do to change them,
so he omits the soldiers.

Now all that remains of his painting is the sky
and the sea
and the castle in the distance
and the trees rolling across the hills
and a few horses grazing in the meadow.

GEORGE BERNARD SHAW

Left Dublin for London when he was twenty,
spidery legs, red nose, large protruding ears,
and crowned with a thatch of reddish hair.
And he was severely afflicted with words
in a fine Irish brogue that kept him a stranger:
"Then he said. . .then she said. . .then this, then that"
Words born in his blood like cells.
Words that wouldn't stay in his mouth.

And constantly writing in little notebooks,
sat in train stations writing. . .writing
political theories and men and women,
horses and wagons and coaches and people,
one with a face like a Member of Parliament,
one who would certainly swing from the gallows.
A slop bucket dumped from an upstairs window,
live birds for sale. . .dead fish for sale. . .
a pickpocket caught in the act,
a woman sleeping in a doorway,
a dead horse lying in the street,
apples and nuts and melons and vegetables,
the smell of bread. . .the smell of spices. . .
and organ grinder and laughing and shouting. . .
words, words, endless words.

Joined a group of well-meaning cranks
who were trying to make society better,
but when he was called on to make a speech
he trembled and sputtered and finally sat down.
But indefatigable Shaw
became a second Demosthenes,
made Socialist speeches in the park
to any gathering of cats and dogs
or nannies pushing their baby buggies
or visionaries starved for a vision.
Once in the rain to a group of police
who were sent there to keep law and order.

Soon he was being paid to make speeches
by groups of ladies and stone-faced men
to show them the way in such terrible times.
With his Irish brogue and terms of endearment
he caught some bright and cheery girls
and some passionate, sullen and somber ones,
all easier to attract than get rid of
till he married Charlotte, the light of his life
who was easy to live with and rather rich.

His novels were dull and wouldn't fly. But his plays!
He made characters live with ideas and humor,
using chessmen to practice their movements on stage:
Major Barbara, The Devil's Disciple,
Pygmalion, Caesar and Cleopatra,
on and on, writing and writing, older and older.

Then, when he was ninety-four,
he fractured his leg while pruning a tree
and was given orders to stay in bed,
everyone saying, "Lie still! Don't move!"
But he always did what he wanted to
so he said, "Well then, I'm going to die!"
and he shut his eyes and did.

AFTER THE RUBAIYAT

In Naishapur, where Omar once had lived,
the men lay on mosaic patios thinking blue and gold
thinking oasis waterfalls under the giant stars,
lay on their sprawling couches
singing of the wilderness to their perfect women,
and of bread and wine just as old Khayam had sung,
that maker of tents and weaver of words,
singing of a young girl fashioned from a silver rib
freshly plucked from the slumbering moon.

But the peaceful envoys of Genghis Khan
visited this city of geometric art
only to have their beards or heads cut off.
The loyal hordes of the Great Khan
galloped out of China lost in dust clouds of revenge,
rushed across the patios slashing the singing throats
and raping the perfect ivory-legged women
until, as in Herat and Samarkand, only Mongolians
and screaming women and quiet, blood-stained scimitars
remained of what had once been Naishapur.

In time these eastern men of flame and sword
who massacred the Persians and devoured their horses
were domesticated by the women they had conquered,
were trained for fathering sons and building mosques
until now maybe a Mongolian word or two,
here and there a set of slanted eyes
and voices somewhat more like frogs than birds
are the only remaining hints of Genghis Khan.

GLENN MILLER

Were you there? Do you remember
how the audience in the Central Theater wept
the last time, the last performance
before Glenn Miller went to war?
Maybe the last time ever.
The saxophones had lumps in their golden throats.
The trumpets, muted and already far away,
made Chattanooga Choo Choo sound like Armageddon,
sound enough like troop trains, war and death
to drive the female vocalist from the stage.
And then the final Moonlight Serenade rose up
to join the stars of that New Jersey sky

Britain was bright at first. Major Glenn Miller,
handsome in his gabardines, became an officer overnight.
Buzz-bombs suddenly erasing houses
came as a surprise — as though he thought
war wasn't really war — just uniforms and music.
But he was on a roll then. Couldn't lose at poker,
organized a band and played for army personnel,
jazzed American Patrol and Volga Boatman
and Johnny Comes more like Swinging Home Again.

But when the officers were told of nuclear devices,
months before one dropped, his luck ran out.
A million fire bombs fell all at once.
Lost weight until his uniform hung loose,
found fault with every member of the band,
and never won another game of poker.

When the band was booked to play in Paris
he tried to get there first, get out of Britain
where the bombs were falling much too close.
All planes were grounded by a dense December fog.
He found a man who had to fly to France,
found a pilot who didn't think that freezing fog
could turn a single-engine plane to ice,
and finally found the death that had been stalking him
ever since that last New Jersey show.

FUGUE

In the land of the raised fist
the brandished rifle, the knife in the teeth
the screaming through streets of minaret and mosque
to keep alive the ancient hates
one man abandons for a day
those idiotic acts of history
and follows his neglected path
through narrow streets of donkeys and shops

to the silken rooms of his black-haired woman,
her eyes of camel and sand
of stars of flame in the dome of night
and speaks to her of a fertile oasis
as she draws the shade and shuts the door.

In the land of toppled statues and the iron rose,
of formations of bombers in the perfect sky,
of parades of ponderous bombs through the square,
through the closely guarded streets,
one man ignores for awhile
the stupid seriousness of history
and goes with longing in his eyes
through streets of laundry and Slavic steeples
through neighborhoods of onion-shaped roofs
to the dark varnished room of his heavy-thighed woman
her eyes of samovars and hardwood forests
of lake ice cracking in the spring
and speaks to her of stars on the Volga
as she draws the shade and shuts the door.

In the land of crowded subways and highway rush
of news of wars and soldiers somewhere else
and security under the missile-webbed skies
one man forsakes for a day
the frightening twists of history
and goes, as he's been wanting to,
through streets of traffic and flashing signs
through neighborhoods of fenced-in lawns
and house-broken dogs and secretive cats
to the tidy rooms of his cluttered woman,
her eyes of typewriters and drug store breakfasts
of dances danced and evenings alone
and speaks to her of a lake in Wisconsin
as she draws the shade and shuts the door.

ITALIAN POETRY READING

One by one the poems were being read —
some boldly and matter-of-fact,
some scowlingly dramatic,
some frightened, almost inaudible.
But all with melodic, flowing words,
words that had more music than meaning
because I knew so little Italian.
Words with roots in my own prehistory.
Words that were silk against my face.

The clatter of dishes, the kitchen voices
the onstantly roaring espresso machine
were background sounds to be overcome.
We should have gathered somewhere in Rome,
maybe next to Trevi Fountain
or by the pines I've never seen.

Now and then a word I knew —
the word for a star...the word for sky,
until I felt I belonged to these people,
knew what their musical sounds were saying —
that they worship the world as I worship the world
with words, saying springtime, mountain and sea,
primavera...montagna...mare,
with all the wonder the world's first people
felt when they named such things.

They've been up in their attics long after dark
praising the world by guttering candlelight,
praising creation with words...words...
saying, "Look! It's me! I'm here! I've seen!"
telling us all about mountains and sky
or the river or "this woman I know"
or "my lover has gone." And always the words.
Or it might have been only the sound of the words,
or the voices and its deep emotions.

But their words were not just sunshine to bask in
or rain to be washed by or thoughts to feed on.
Their words were contagious. They clung to me.
When I left, though I barely knew what they meant,
they followed me down the street.

DELIUS

As though on a pilgrimage to some holy place
he, like the Old Man of the Sea on Sinbad's back,
had his family and servants carry him,
his fierce will and bones of a bird
and the raging disease that was reaming him out,
bitching, bitching all the way
up, up, up the high mountain,
up the foggy trail through the vapors of morning
to the very peak where he could turn his face
this way and that and up and around
to see with his eyes
and feel with his flesh
and absorb in his brain the source of creation,
the first light from the pure sun of knowing.

If there were celestial choirs there,
harmonics he had never written
or counterpoint he might never conceive,
they were for his ears, for his blood alone.
But all the way back through the layers of living,
down the steeps paths of frost and sweat,
there were no words spoken,
only the constant scraping of feet
and the sound of exhausted breathing.

And back once again in his valley home
where they placed him in bed like a small sacrifice,
he stared at the ceiling all night long
and through the remaining days of his life
had the look of a man who was still on his mountain.

JEAN SIBELIUS

He was born bald and he died bald.
When he was young, when his hair was thick,
he wrote powerful music that sounded like Finland
and talked with anyone who would listen
about his music and all of his theories —
the colors of music, the music of things.
Then click! he'd switch to his other self,
his violin under his chin all day,
stand on a rock and play to the forest,
on the prow of a boat and play to the sea.
"That tree is Finland. That lake is Finland.
The sky, and even I, are Finland."

But when he was halfway through his life
Time, playing the role of Delilah,
discovered that he, like the biblical Samson
owed his strength to his full head of hair.
So little by little, day by day
plucked one here, a couple there
until his head was as barren and smooth
as any rock on the shores of Finland.
Along with his hair went his love of music —
no more composing and no more talk.
He never allowed his daughters to sing
and built a soundproof room in the basement.
Smiled at the crowds who cheered for his music
but never knew what to say.

REGINALD MARSH

Artists for parents, paint in his chromosomes.
Programmed to live the life he led.
He never painted a duck or a chicken
and all of his horses were carousel horses,
nostrils flared, eyes fierce and straining,
mouths stretched open to shriek their cry.
And always the beautiful, full-figured women
in casual control of the beasts they ride,
their facial expressions like empty rooms.

He painted the strippers in burlesque shows.
Or down in Jimmy Kelly's saloon,
painted the lonely dancer,
painted the inaccessible nudity,
the tranquilized beauty in her face
having her always the dominant figure,
princess over the shabby men
who ponder her through smoke and lust.

Though his was the greatest lust of all,
this paintaholic of hundreds of notebooks,
the pencil or brush a part of his hand
to help capture, help worship, the perfect woman.
He searched The Bowery and Coney Island,
the side shows, and mostly the beach. . .the beach.
The buxom girls, their faces gone wandering,
perched on the shoulders of musclebound boyfriends.
Their bright colors offset the drabness
of destitute streets and conquered people
or imparted life to the crowds he'd paint.
His women — the strength of marathon dances.
Their shoulders — pillows for sleeping men.

His sketchbooks chronicled his time —
the breadlines, the headlines, the uniforms,
tugboats, the opera, and cheap hotels —

all that was part of New York, New York.
Addicted to alcohol, hooked on paint,
and quietly, constantly worshipping crowds
that included his beautiful, vacuous women.
Then, when burlesque shows all closed down
or were driven across the line to New Jersey,
he followed them there and died.

SERGEI IN CONCERT

Strictly suit and tie, Rachmaninoff,
head in the clouds and extra long arms
draped over the keys in a simian way,
each hand an octave and a half
playing preludes, etudes and sonatas,
rhapsodies and variations
until slowly, gradually, we discover
the orchestra is always Russia,
the piano always Rachmaninoff
in conflict with the sounds of Russia.

The orchestra is always Russia:
its fields and forests, rivers and lakes,
its horizons of farms, its cities of people,
its soldiers marching through the night streets,
its guns and tanks and unbendable purpose,
its solid, Slavic liturgies,
its heavy brooding Russian love,
tender moon and violent earth
crowded out by its iron life .
Its sadness the melancholy eye
of a huge, captured animal
all streaked through the blood of the orchestra
that enchants or caresses or tortures Rachmaninoff
who answers, but only through the piano.

He plays his interpretations of Russia:
the background music of Chaplin movies,
music to skate by, to view plastic flowers by,
to dance on the backs of elephants by
or march into blazing machine guns by,
for weeping by banks of a blood-stained river
or watching one's love marry someone else.
Resigned to the memory of what has been,
frantic with fear over what is to come,
He is Rachmaninoff, Rachmaninoff,
the boy who practiced and practiced piano
until it became his only voice.
When he changed his citizenship he died.

ROLE-MODEL DREAM

What's happened? All of a sudden I'm Paul Gauguin,
Put on my hat and walk out of the office,
the books out of balance, but I don't care.
Put on my hat and walk out of the house,
say I'm buying a paper, but never come back.
Take one last look at Gilmore Heights,
its identical houses, its men in black suits.
A one-legged stork perched on every roof.
A pink flamingo on every lawn.
Dogs named "Spot" and cats named "Tabby."

Soon I'm on some sleepy island
where buxom girls carry things on their heads
and sun-blackened men pull the ropes of a fishnet,
me with only the clothes on my back
and my bottomless bundle of paint jars and canvas.
In time, almost deja-vulike, I find
just as Gauguin had found on Tahiti,
the model I'll paint so incessantly,
my Tehura of the expressive hands,

the sun on the waves behind her eyes
as she walks with her aura of ancestors.
Her skin is the color of wet sand.
Her face reflects the soul of the island.

I paint her by a pond in the woods,
on the sun-swept beach or the moon-soaked pier,
dressed as a queen or a cleaner of fish,
paint her brown or blue or pink or green,
paint her high in the sky floating upside down
wearing only leaves or braided flowers,
paint her carrying laundry on her head,
paint her asleep as a form of praise,
paint her young as she was or old as she will be.

But then, during this cyclone of painting,
I study her as she lies on the sand
seeming clear one moment, blurred the next.
Maybe the sun. Or overwork.
She fades away, leaving me on the beach,
leaving me alone in Gilmore Heights
with its storks and flamingos and men in black suits
and "Tabbys" and "Spots" and identical houses,
leaving me my back-and-forth train,
alone in my office of ledgers and balance sheets
sorting debits from credits, living from dream .

But I often think of our time together,
that our hut on the island is being discovered
and all those paintings of my stay there
are blinding everyone with their brilliance,
and I half expect that someday soon
I'll be back there painting Tehura.

SERGEI ESENIN

In Moscow, in the big city,
he enchanted tavern crowds with his poetry
his accordion, his young face and blond curly hair,
reciting memories of old wooden Russia
gleaned from his Bible of the winds,
storks nesting in the chimneys,
the sky a bright blue scarf for the birches,
the woods and rivers and dusty roads.

Yes, he married Isadora Duncan,
caught the Firebird by the tail.
Or did Isadora marry him, she on the brink of fifty,
she whose children had recently drowned?
How else could she take him along to America
where she had been booked to dance?

And yes, he drank, becoming almost degenerate,
stole her money and smashed her mirrors,
streaked naked through the hotel lobby
and gave her lavish clothes away.
Their violent fights and tender apologies,
for the first time he wrote of love.
It was Iron Russia he had been fighting,
the foundries and factories and steel fist.
The collapse of the past. The uprooted past.
"The stern October has deceived me."
She loved him and called him Golden Head.

Then, so very old but barely thirty,
he went to visit his native village
where the young men were singing different songs,
a foreigner in his own home town,
like "the windmill with one wing left to wave."

And that was the end of his Wooden Russia,
the end of his love for the aging dancer
except for some details he had to attend to —
a suicide poem he wrote with his blood
and hanging himself in the closet.

THE LONG BOATS

Sing, now, of the Viking men
the written word has kept alive,
the dusty Copenhagen sagas
that tell of Greenland and Eric the Red,
how they sailed west in their broad-beamed ships.
West, the magnet that tugs at the blood —
dragon-head prows to frighten off monsters,
bright colored sails billowing out
and waves slapping the clinker-built hulls
that faded away in the ocean's haze.
Quiet, though now and then someone shouting,
maybe calling out North Star directions
or, half drunk on fermented fruit,
shouting the words of some runic tune
or bellowing, "All's well!"

I should sing of how Vikings landed in Vinland
mistaking a continent for an island,
how they found apples and rabbit and deer
and tall pines that sang of home
like the blonde-haired voices last heard in Sweden.

And the wild daughter of Eric the Red,
how she and her ineffective husband
went along on one of the voyages,
were attacked by Indians, probably Iroquois
somewhere up in the wooded hills,
how she ripped off the top of her tunic,
grabbed the sword of a fallen Viking
and struck her breasts, screaming a
wild Valkyrie cry that sent the Indians
running in fear to their birch canoes.

And I'd sing of the following five hundred years
when West was a terror, the edge of the world.
History slept and the air was clean

for the rabbits and deer and the self-sown grain
until even larger ships loomed from the sea.
Then I'd sing of the five hundred years after that,
then finally give up that ridiculous harp
and almost impossible songs.

MR. BECK'S BOOKSTORE

The door chimes go for hours without ringing
but he acts as though customers are there
quietly browsing, drawing life from the books
like hummingbirds sipping flowers.
Or like lonely eavesdroppers in a restaurant
consuming scattered fragments of sentences.

Though obviously knowing he's alone
walled-in by the smell of aging books —
some with mildew, some with broken spines,
red and brown and orange and white and green —
Lady Chatterly...Virgil...Stonewall Jackson...
withering on their shelves,
slipping away from life like neglected pets,
like old friends whose features have turned thick,
growing gradually more distant.

A tree that falls unheard in its forest
makes a sound like an unread book.
A woman who sees her lover off to war
knows the feeling of aloneness.
The murmur of old books clinging to life
makes the bookstore hum like a seashell.
Some release chariots in the air
that slowly fade away like smoke.
Some hold stately women and pirates and kings
locked between their drying covers
waiting for them to die.

What a fire they would make,
a recycling of book back to spirit.
Except then there'd be failure, a great waste
as the bookstore crumbles to the ground
and the hoped-for freeing of characters
writhing up phoenix-like from the ashes
might just be the rage of the fire-eyed authors.
Some spent their entire lives on a book,
sometimes even died for a book,
writing with a mixture of ink and blood.
But none of them ever considered failure.
No book ever written to die on a shelf.
So, brave as a book, he'll stay with his bookstore
till they dry up together and blow away.

WINSTON CHURCHILL

One third bulldog, two thirds man
symbol of the British Empire.
Born in ancient Blenheim Palace.
Not a bit like Merry England
with its noisy music halls
and bawdy ballads in the pubs.
More like dungeons, ghosts and cobwebs.
Winston Churchill — sprung from rock

Squeaked through military school,
arguing with his professors —
bad grades and attitude.
Served his army time in India
playing polo. . .playing polo.
Then, like an owl looking down
observing Africa's Boer War,
learning warfare on the scene,
master of the gun and pen.
Another war, this time in Cuba

fighting on the Spanish side.
Climbed the Military ladder
controversy all the way.
Swords can't win against machine guns.
Time to mobilize the Navy.

The two world wars were really one
with twenty years time out for thinking,
time for calmly painting pictures,
even time for growing soldiers.
Churchill's vow: to rescue England.
"I was put on earth for that."

Played Europe like a game of chess,
the ocean like an organ.
First we'll knock out Italy,
stab Europe in its underbelly.
Bring in all the heavy guns,
a victory...some losses there.
But not a thought for deep mud
or mine fields...or night attacks.
Not a thought for stray bombs
or skulls on the battle fields
shining in the sun.
Or empty places at the table...
Empty beds upstairs.
Or brave men in hospitals...
that's to be expected.
It's a young man's duty
to go marching off to war.
"From defeat to defeat," he said,
disaster to disaster,
catastrophe to catastrophe
until the war is won."
Then, as Churchill walked away
he passed a battered butterfly and wept

ISADORA DUNCAN

Born broke in the San Francisco hills
thirty years after the lust for gold,
out of the cradle endlessly dancing
to ocean waves and random winds
running and bending and pausing and floating
to streams of music that flow forever,
to delicatessens and butcher shops,
flute and lyre and horn and harp,
Chopin, Mozart and Satie,
dancing the course her life is to take,
up and up and down and down,
bright waves on fathomless water.

Cloven-hoofed piper drawing her on
to rickety stages and music halls
and a doddering cattle boat to London.
Dance without music...Dance without shoes...
Berlin, Vienna and Budapest
suddenly merging from girl to woman,
white tunic and golden sandals,
showers of sunlight and lilies on water,
scenery of Greek and Egyptian temples
and endless cries of "Isadora!"
as young men of the audience
remove the horses from her carriage
and pull her, sing to her through the streets.

From a chronically love-sick begetter of children
receiving a daughter,
form and movement...emotion as force...
tambourines and jangling bells.
From a kindly old millionaire, a son,
always dance upward...never dance down...
pipes and drums and concertinas
constantly raging through her blood.

The children! The children! The beautiful children!
They with their little leapings and runnings
until the automobile they're in
rolls backward into the River Seine,
drowned like kittens in a sack.

After that the bad days come dancing,
tumbling and clattering over each other
and all the hours and days and years
with their sorrows and regret drift by
until dance becomes religion,
its church, her school for little girl dancers. . .
Sibelius and Mendelssohn. . .Bartok and Bach. . .
she, the priestess, floats through the air
with all the neophyte Isadorables
hopping and leaping behind her.

Her dancing school for children in Moscow,
the agile grace of her marble body
motion springing from emotion
until she marries a Russian poet
just for the music of his words,
little pancake and caviar man
who follows her halfway around the world
with all his absurdity and tears,
writes his last poem with blood from his wrists
and hangs himself in the hotel closet

while Isadora. . .Isadora
dancing with veils or without,
dances her way to the French Riviera
where her scarf makes love to a racing car's wheel
and ends her dancing forever.

GEORGIO de CHIRICO

*If you don't fit into the world you're in,
create a world where you do.*
— *Anonymous Wise Man*

Born in Greece where the treasured ruins
mingled hopelessly with his being.
Then, in Italy, infected by ancient statues,
gladiators who fought to the death,
towering clocks and shattered columns
and huge horses with long flowing manes,
all seen through his extraterrestrial eyes,
all painted from his desperate melancholy.

"I've never seen horses like that," said Magritte.
A dream horse with a horse's soul."
"Nor a nude like those," said vaux.
"Nor a still life as vibrant as this one," said Ernst.
And Salvador Dali and Yves Tanguy
seeing everyday things for the very first time.

But renouncing his style, he said, "I am de Chirico,
the last of the classical renaissance painters."
They called him a coward...called him a traitor,
held a surrealist funeral for him
because he refused to relinquish the past.
Rooted, like Italy, in the past.

But what sort of life was this?
Ninety years of painting...painting...
hardly more than a paint brush and brain.
Had a sense of destiny all his life
feeling something big was about to happen.
But to live in the past is to know the past
where Venice was the only surprise,
always sinking but never sinks.

He painted his model, who never grew old,
the fall of her hair. . .the tilt of her chin. . .
her eyes on the edge of infinity.
Painted faceless people with egg-shaped heads
and painted self-portraits over and over,
an unbroken history of himself,
de Chirico nude or at his easel,
painted himself in various costumes,
17th Century. . .18th Century. . .
Painted himself with a bust of Minerva.
To paint thyself is to know thyself.

But for all his painting nothing happened
until the clock reached its programmed hour
for his lavender soul to slip away,
perhaps to be born again in the present
so that any day now he might paint the scene
of seagulls following his boat
as it slowly sailed into the past

FRANK

On the beach not far from his home,
Pablo Picasso and several children
drew their pictures in the sand —
sad-eyed minotaurs, bearded warriors
and, of course, a ripe young girl —
drew with sticks or with their fingers
working carefully and fast,
laughing at each addition they made,
at every ludicrous innovation,
laughed as they raced the rising tide,
seagulls flying by to scream,
dolphins calling from the water.
Their laughing ended as they watched
the first wave lap the warrior's feet,

the second eat the young girl's legs,
watched as one by one the waves
washed their preposterous art away
making the beach seem smaller and clean
as though their art had never been.

Like fat Frank in our high school class
drawing, drawing, always drawing
any two-legged, four-legged, no-legged thing.
Poor at everything but art.
Prolific charcoal. Insatiable brush.
Wore a blue tam to look the part.

There were several empty houses then,
mortgage defaults and that sort of thing.
No vandalism. No destruction,
except for the house on Catalpa Street
where Frank got past the kitchen door
and used the plaster walls for canvas.
Rembrandt or Michelangelo
guided his hand as it held the brush.
Painted an owl that looked down from its tree,
the moon in its phases, birds busy thinking,
Arabian dancers in filmy skirts.
And blue women eating together,
green men lying in the sun.
Bright birds, speckled fish,
green lizards, silver snakes,
everything brilliant. . .everything flying
while people kept walking by, not knowing.

But as certain as waves, as sure as tides
the house was sold and bolted shut
and all its walls of life and color
were sloshed as bare as a tide-swept beach
making the rooms seem smaller and clean
as though his art had never been.

"GUERNICA"

Pablo Picasso, for most of his life,
had a screaming, dying horse in his head
left over from watching, when he was a boy,
a bull in the ring as it gored a horse.
He often painted a wounded horse,
the innocent victim of every corrida.
And he constantly painted the crucifixion,
Christ on the cross and gored in the side,
thirty-nine such works in fifty-six years.
The horse, the crucifixion, the bull,
all symbols of innocent victims,
cluttering Picasso's brain.

Guernica, "Sacred Town of the Basques"
sheep and goats and eggs and cheese,
and testing ground for modern weapons.
Born before the Romans and Goths,
died on an April afternoon
from two hours of one-ton bombs
and various incendiaries,
Franco's Junkers and Heinkel bombers
reduced Guernica to a field of rubble.
The Loyalists asked him to paint a mural
to show everyone what the fascists had done.

Within a month of that clinical bombing,
he made forty-five studies and eight revisions,
represented the world in black and white,
as the world is seen through the eyes of an animal.
The bull looking on, bewildered,
as though it just wandered onto the scene
amazed, as always, at human behavior.
And the wounded, screaming, dying horse,
dying, as always, the innocent victim.
The butchered warrior spread out on the ground,

Guernica

a Picasso crucifix toppled over.
The burning woman at the right
screams out her anguish of physical pain.
The bereaved woman at the left
screams out at the loss of her dead child.
A woman's head and the lamp she is holding
wreathes through a window observing the scene
as a woman had watched the crucifixion,
as women witness death in the bull ring.
A small flower springs up from the rubble,
a symbol of hope, the persistence of life.
All that had littered Picasso's brain
swept onto one enormous canvas
to describe the meaningless murder of Guernica.
The painting could have been called "Picasso."

PABLO NERUDA
*To paint the sky you must
keep your feet on the ground."*

He read in taverns, read to students,
to the old who carry their eyes in pouches
and children bright with life.
Read in streets and factories and gardens,
in city squares, union halls and mines,
in Genoa, Cuba, New York and Brazil
to people thirsty for poetry.
"Read to us, Pablo! Read some more!"
Perched on the window sills, hunched on the floors,
in the aisles or on each other's laps,
their ears strained, their eyes lost.
Neruda — lover of women and words.
"I came to <u>live</u> in this world," he said.
Read in a Guatamala jail, machine guns aimed at him
in case his poems got out of line.

A collector of things he could see or touch —
the flotsam of shipwrecks — bottles and furniture,
prow figureheads of sea-pocked wood,
brass fittings and instruments.
He held long dialogues with the ocean,
devoted to things that could shape his life —
words and ideas, laughter and friends.
Enjoyed bringing lovers together.
Had a way of seeing the world in words.

"It was years before I finally learned
that what I was writing was poetry."
Those who remembered and knew him,
who wrote in their solitary rooms,
in the dark corners of restaurants,
on fast trains, in parked cars,
picnic benches or anchored boats,
who wrote as they lived remembering him
were loosely or firmly bound to him
by umbilical rays of invisible light
as though he were some sort of blazing sun,
some nourishing force for them to draw on.

Defying the rigid dictatorship
crowds followed his funeral through the streets.
His closest friend said, "Honor his passing
with a wild moment of laughter and shouting."
But Pablo Neruda himself had said,
"I would gladly come back from far away
just to leave again — a kind of dying."

Say anything you want, but it's the words that sing. They soar and descend...I bow to them...love them, cling to them. I run them down, bite into them, melt them down...I love words so much — the unexpected ones, the ones I wait for greedily or stalk until, suddenly, they drop.

Vowels I love. They glitter like colored stones. They leap like silver fish. They are foam, thread, metal, dew. I run after certain words. They are so beautiful that I want to fit them all into my poems. I catch them in mid-flight, as they buzz past. I trap them, clean them, peel them. I set myself in front of the dish. They have a crystalline texture to me, vibrant, ivory, vegetable, oily — like fruit, like algae, like agates, like olives. And then I mash them, garnish them, let them go. I leave them in my poem like stalactites, like slivers of polished wood, like coats, pickings from a shipwreck, gifts from the waves. Everything exists in the word. An idea goes through a complete change because one word shifted its place, or because another settled down like a spoiled little thing inside a phrase that was not expecting her, but obeys her. They have shadow, transparence, weight, feathers, hair, and everything they gathered from so much rolling down the river, from so much wandering from country to country, from being roots so long. They are very ancient and very new. They live in the coffin, hidden away, and in the budding flower.

What a great language I have. It's a fine language we inherited from the fierce *conquistadores*. They strode over the giant cordilleras, over the rugged Americas, hunting for potatoes, sausages, beans, tobacco, gold, corn, fried eggs, with a voracious appetite not found in the world since then. They swallowed up everything — religions, pyramids, tribes, idolatries — just like the ones they brought along in their huge sacks. Wherever they went they razed the land. But words fell like pebbles out of the boots of the barbarians, out of their beards, their helmets, their horseshoes, luminous words that were left glittering here...our language. We came up losers...We came up winners...They carried off the gold and left us the gold...They carried everything off and left us everything...They left us the words.

Pablo Neruda, *Memoirs*,
Farrar, Straus and Giroux, 1976

LUDWIG CON BRIO

Ludwig van Beethoven, peasant stock —
Dutch roots transplanted in Germany.
Like Vincent van Gogh and Salvador Dali,
named for an infant brother who died.
Like Mozart and Nicolo Paganini,
forced by his father to practice, practice —
his alcoholic, nagging father
who rubbed his hands at the thought of money,
driving moody young Ludwig to tears.

Quartets, concertos, sonatas and fugues,
G Minor, D Minor, E flat and C —
each a prediction of greater things
but nothing outstanding until he reached thirty.
Thought of himself as a prince in disguise,
respected money but worshipped power:
Napoleon, his Eroica hero.

Beethoven, always in ludicrous love
with ideal ephemeral woman —
from high society, of course —
usually young and slender and soulful,
a pupil or someone recently met
who would wreathe up from his magic piano
like a vision, an image shaped in smoke.
But all in his head and always hopeless.
Proposed to Magdalene, then to Theresa;
his best compositions followed rejection.

He could hypnotize a stone with his music,
improvising songs of love.
Enchanted several stone-hearted women

Beethoven

but when his music died away
they'd describe him as being short and ugly.
Pock-marked face and rude behavior,
out of step if he tried to dance,
stumbling on furniture, stepping on feet.
Add to this his growing deafness —
conversed with scribbled scraps of paper.
No wonder he had a quick temper —
Drank jovial wine in the local tavern
but one wrong word would murder a friendship.

He worked with sounds he couldn't hear,
locked up in a world he had made for himself.
Every emotional wound he suffered
hemorrhaged its share of fugues and sonatas.
He had to be turned around to see
how wildly the audience was applauding
his Ninth and final symphony.
He died during a violent thunderstorm.
Maybe he heard it — maybe not.

THE WHITE GULL AND THE COW'S FAT TONGUE

Nothing of this day escapes me —
not the chemistry of Annie,
not her face,
not her touch,
out in the yard this morning,
down in the tall grass this afternoon,
then in the restaurant,
and now in the dark cavern theater
with its ceiling of stars and plaster angels.

But the wide vision screen is tearing me from her
with its casual horror and almost automatic death
of this Lorca. . .

this Garcia Lorca.
The brutish Guardia Civil,
crazed with the madness of Spain,
is breaking into the house
where his friends have been hiding him,
where he sits reading,
where candles carve dark from his corner of the room,
and he, only vaguely aware of his destiny.

Now they lead him away at gunpoint,
past the dog snarling in the street,
past the horse rotting in the field,
up the mountain path to a place of trees
where he digs his own grave in the fine rain,
in the drizzle of evening.
The branches of a dead tree
stretch out like an unused nervous system.
Only two senseless shots are needed
to release all the poems locked in his head.

The lobster screams in the boiling water.
The harpoon wrings a plaintive squeal
from the great white whale.
Only in death does the giraffe cry out.
But with Lorca it is not the surprise of the bullet
nor the surprise of death,
but the surprise that any man wished him dead.

The projector grinds over us in the dark
like a faint roll of drums.
Annie sits beside me with heaven in her blouse
The Guardia Civil in the bloated night
levels the grave of Garcia Lorca.
And I, I am the world spinning forever
between Venus and Mars,
between Annie warm and close to the sun
and Garcia Lorca dead from war,
whirling out in the cold edge of the universe
through the dizziness of years.

d.a. levy

If only he could have sung to the tune
of flutes in a sheep-pocked meadow
or shouted along with the drums and cymbals
of some colorful, festival street
instead of being wedged in with juvenile singers
strangling on unheard protest songs
in their huddled backroom espresso house
there in that East Cleveland desert.

When he wrote poems to make them happy
they sat giggling between their legs
at his treating words like prostitutes,
at the way he recited four-letter obscenities.
He took Morning Glory seeds, acid, and grass
and they came to acquire the status of hearing
a real live drug scene poet.
Whenever he wrote in anger they laughed
and police began asking to see his draft card
asking, "Why can't you work like everyone else?"

He was all fires and protest riots
that bubbled over into his blood,
wrenched at the bars of his prison brain
as he roared through the empty Cleveland streets.
The ancient houses turned away,
their doors nailed shut with fear.
The sterile concrete towers looked down
dying of lysol in their halls.

But the people he felt so compelled to lift up —
he'd forgotten how much they had to be lied to,
how conditioned they were to reject their feelings,
how bewildered they were by love without money,
how isolated they were from the moon.

So he conjugated his life into poems
there in that shack of a refuge, THE WELL
where the kids were letting their hair grow long
and coffee and cokes and Miles Davis music
were the big underground sins of their time.

It was there that the staunch city fathers came,
their surveillance eyes straining through the walls
until the coffee house refuge died.
They nailed the Stars and Stripes to the door
as a symbol of righteous victory
and danced like councilman gods in the street
as levy, beneath the black skies of winter,
threw up on the frozen wordless ground.
He could never quite assimilate
the aggregate souls who lived in his eyes,
the phantoms with television auras,
the policemen dreaming of flag-wrapped death,
the young girls saying, "I know what I've got
and how much love I can buy,"
or the matador turned stockroom clerk
gored by his unrelenting ulcer.

And all the time, the poems...the poems,
but he, grown so weary of hearing,
"What do you mean? What do you mean?"
that he really didn't know anymore.
He said, "They have something to do with love,"
and wrapped them up as you'd wrap a fish
and left them on a publisher's doorstep,
little bastards that they were.
That was the tragedy —
to be able to carry his entire life
in his arms, all in one small package.

And then,
 with nothing left but the famine in him,
his shadow gone, his reflection gone,

he put a bullet through his head
and all his as yet unwritten words
oozed out to stain the rubber streets.
Train commuters looked up from their papers,
drivers glanced up as they raced by,
planes overhead beamed down their observance,
and the old faces in the park
registered their dull disapproval
saying, "What are you doing on our street?"

But what else could he do?
How could he go on feeding poems
to people hungering for blood
in this industrial, pre-holocaust age?
He was tired of watching the old world die
and knowing that he would even be outlawed,
alive, but screaming in the dark,
in the bright, shining world of tomorrow.

So his puzzled teenage waitress wife
from the lonely all-night death ship restaurant
signed some documents at the morgue
and some friends signed an note for 300 dollars,
the cost of turning a poet to ashes
in Cleveland.

THE RED SHOES

I am writing about this girl
whose walk is more of a skip than a walk
where the leaves blow or the lake roars
or lambs nibble the stubbled grass.
As she hums her content, half-notes slip from her lips.
Quarter-notes curl upward through the air.
Even jammed in a crowd that is more like a river
she stands out by her red hair bouncing.
Even in the office where she types
she walks as though seagulls are in the air
and she barefoot on the shore.

But what ominous portent sort of day is this
that she wanders by a shoestore on Van Buren Street
where swarthy Italian cobbler elf,
his voice the strum of a faint guitar,
reaches out from his tomb of a shop
proffering, offering her these shoes, The Red Shoes!
saying, "You like?" Then Poof! They're on her feet
and he with smoke and flame in his eyes
hops about like a cricket or some crazy bug.

A priest reaches out to hold her back,
clutching at her gauzy skirt,
but The Red Shoes force her to dance
through streets of frantic piano and erotic flute
past blue houses with cats in their windows,
anonymous houses with hollow cheeks.
She dances to her room with its stuffed dog
and souvenir pillows and covered bird cage,
dances through her office turned to jade
with emerald desks and floors of gold,
dances through streets of tolling bells
where her lover glares with icicle eyes.
She dances through the decapitated night
through violent rain and off to the stars

the neighbors at their voyeur windows,
exertion throbbing at her throat.
At dawn her dress reflects the sun.
The clouds drift from their puddles
and drops no longer drip from the eaves.
She dances with newspapers in the streets
as the piano becomes a languid saxophone.

Now things grow hazy. Was it a train
that struck her? Or a truck?
The people standing near wear tired masks
and watch her lie crumpled on the ground,
a string of tears around her neck.
She is supposed to die, but I am writing this.
I decide, No, she will live, and tenderly remove
the Red Shoes from her feet. The crowd smiles.
Flowers bloom in the windows above us.
I take her hand and together we walk somewhere or other,
I haven't decided yet.

ON READING THE LIFE OF JUAN PONCE DE LEON

This was a man as sober as stone.
Or his bones — in the wall of the great cathedral.
For a time, the ruler of Puerto Rico
but all his life the consummate soldier —
wind him up and have him kill.
Brown-nosing the King of Spain
to be ruler of this or ruler of that
until he was struck by a poison arrow
that ended him and his conquest of Florida
which he mistook for a rather large island.

But not a word of the Fountain of Youth
that the Indian baglady told him about —

just sat behind his mahogany desk
or joked about it at cocktail parties
as one more example of gullible Indians.

I'd always thought of him as obsessed —
on his hands and knees like Nebuchadnezzar
clawing the earth for the magic water
to bathe in or drink for eternal youth
so he could be young for his young wife
and no longer leave her for years at a time
to go conquistadoring the world.

Considered him just as mad as Columbus
who sailed away to the brink of the earth.
Or Van Gogh who recreated the sky,
painting the wind as an aberration.
Or someone as daft as the blind Irish poet
who wandered through the emerald hills
thrumming his harp and dredging his songs
up from the constant darkness he lived in,
up from the well of his Gaelic blood.

On this twisted journey we all must make
there are plenty of men who run to the king
saying, "Make me this or make me that,
give me the paper that gives me power..."
while their wives stay home in their empty houses
waiting through the prime of their lives.
Ah, Ponce de Leon — thy dreamy eyes
were just as shifty as the rest.

CAPRICCIO

Convinced that death is preferable to this,
Tchaikovsky wandered off to drown himself
in the October waters of the Moscow River
unaware he'd thus abort such things
as Sleeping Beauty, Nutcracker, or Pathetique.
But the ice slivers and the night's cold
were harsher than the world at its worst,
than his hatred for the woman he'd married
or the constant loneliness that drew him there.

So squishing home, drenched to the hips, he became
the patron saint of all failed suicides
who tease death in a thousand ways,
teetering on the cliff's brink or roof's edge,
pouring potions in their drinks,
or holding pistols to their heads
but never jumping nor swallowing the poison,
or firing the gun. Never lounging too long
on river bottoms or under the lily pads.
Always ludicrous, unruffled by failure,
but never taking life seriously again.

STREETS OF NOBLE BIRTH

I feel compelled to burn a book. Any book.
An orange one. One I've never read.
Act like it might be harmful to the mind
or prompt one to commit unpleasant acts,
so get rid of it.
See to it that no one has a chance to read it. Ever.

So I take a book from the shelf at random
Don't look at it — smuggle it from the house
like stealing silver, or kidnapping the cat.
I take it to the vacant lot across the street,
kneel on the ground and spread it like a tent,
then lean over it and strike a match.
It's a day in autumn with the leaves still green
though some already brown with death have fallen.
When a car passes by I act nonchalant,
like someone fond of nature. . .someone watching birds.

Don't know the book's name or who the author is,
yet as the match flares up I'm Abraham in the wilderness
sacrificing Isaac his only son.
The foggy trees surround me, The imaginary ram relieved
to learn the fire is for the book, not him
and no big winged angel comes to stop me.
Maybe the angel is the wind that blows out the first match.
I strike another and a page or two catch fire.
A crow shrieks from the tree above.

I smile.
I have added one more credit to my name: Book Burner!
I am head of the Ministry of Education.
A member of the Library Board.
I am Mr. Tightcollar, never looking right nor left
on my street called Straight.
Lock my daughter in a tower.
Make my wife wear high-necked dresses.

The pages only half burn and go out.
I light the book again. Hunch over it.
Shield it from the angel wind.
But something I hadn't planned on happens —
I read one of its half-burned sentences:
> "Georgianne, her eyes of sampans on the Yellow Sea,
> of guitars crying out in their loneliness."

That was a mistake.
I should have thumbed through this book first,
chosen some almanac to burn, some book of no feeling,
some book of dead statistics or an old phone book.
I should have tossed it in the furnace and slammed the door
like dropping a bomb from the air onto a row of houses.
Such things should be sudden and impersonal.
But not seen.
Never look your victim in the eye.
The flame has gone out again.
The book is only one third burned, but I have to finish .
It dies like Rasputin — bullets, poison, clubbing, stabbing
and still staggering, driven by some spirit in it.
I lean over to relight the pages,
cup the match in my hand,
shelter the flame from the wind until it catches.
I watch more sentences as they turn to ash:
> "Harold jabs his cigarette in the egg left on his plate
> revealing his innate disregard for life."

Why do I burn this book?
Who am I to be burning this book?
What do I expect to find —
lurid pages cooled off by the flames?
Accounts of Rosemary Cleavage bursting from her blouse,
hopping from bed to bed in just her scanties,
her eyes like black cats of yearning?
Maybe Balkan wedding nights of catsup-soiled sheets
hung from the bedroom window to please the groom
while roars of village laughter shake the hills.

And why am I burning this book here?
Why not on some Walpurgis of black sky,
trees flickering red from the flaming book
and a dozen feverishly fanatic book burners
their faces bright with fire and streaked with charcoal,
dancing their crazy ritual dance?
But not just me alone on an afternoon of autumn
in this vacant lot where I know each monotonous tree and rock.

Now the book is a fragile ghost,
a carcass of crumbling black pages.
Only an edge of the cover still glows red.
But I can read the title: "Streets of Noble Birth."
And shreds of the author's name —
Helen...Something — calm in her martyrdom.
I grind it with my shoe, turning the pages to grains of soot,
spread them around, kick them into the tall weeds,
toss dead leaves over the charred spot on the grass
and walk back across the street.

I think of Helen Whoever-She-Is writing that book,
writing her eyes red up in her attic room,
writing in her backhand scrawl, her Gothic mind
full of ampersands and syntax, Harold and Georgianne,
even as she eats her meals or does her shopping.
I feel her secret pride on seeing strangers read her book.

I feel like washing my hands. And my face.
Feel like buying a copy of that book,
having it hand-bound in tooled leather.
I'd keep it in a special place...a book to be proud of.
Maybe on an end table with elegant bookends to hold it.
I think I'd feel better after that.

EXCAVATION

If they dig us out of lava
will I, guitar in hand, be discovered
standing on the tree stump beneath your window
singing some bawdy serenade
and you, draped over the window sill above,
still giggling and tossing a rose
through the fresh evening lava
much to the disgust of the scandalized neighbors
not as yet dug up?

Or will I,
if they ever dig us out of lave,
be discovered standing guitar in hand,
on the tree stump beneath your window
singing some bawdy serenade in the fresh evening lava
while you, fearful of what
the neighbors not as yet dug up might think,
are discovered sulking in an easy chair
somewhere in the house — hiding from the window,
a wilted rose in your lap,
a dull dead dream in your eye
and a tear on your cheek that looks like amber?

Or, if they ever dig us out of lava,
will all they find be a tree stump in your yard
and you asleep with the window locked
and a guitar full of lava in the closet
somewhere on the other side of town
and me in the kitchen of another house
drinking a stein of lava to forget,
content with the thought that
the neighbors not as yet dug up
may sleep on peacefully and undisturbed?

POETRY READING

They come looking for the bluebird,
for keys to cages they have
locked themselves into,
sit defiant. . .sit expectant. . .
sit pleading "Oil me! Oil me!"
like malfunctioning machines,
their souls in little bottles
hanging at their necks
or dangling from their waists.

They see her standing before them
like a slave girl on the auction block,
her smooth iambics of shoulder and throat,
her sculptured verses of breast and waist,
her rhythmic lines of hip and thigh
and wait for poetry.

Then her voice in the half-light
as startling as a dove at the open window.
They hear salvaged scraps of her living,
wedges of sunlight,
the sparkle of streets,
glissandos of an afternoon,
learn of the adhesion of friendship,
of hands touching and not touching,
of eagles and field mice,
cormorants and fish,
hear the scent and roar and wash of sea,
hear time feeding on its young.

And then, when she finishes and leaves,
some fly along the street beside her,
some ride behind her on horseback
in bright colored capes like Castilian nobles
and some remain in their folding chairs
counting their beads
or staring at spots on the oak floor.